I0490045

TRINITY

THE LOST SECRETS OF PUBLIC SPEAKING AND WHY WE TALK AT ALL

MARTIN SVANEBORG

COPYRIGHT

TALKS *for* CHANGE BOOKS

Talks For Change Books is part of the
Martin Svaneborg brand which can be found at

martinsvaneborgtalks.com

First published world-wide online by Talks for Change Books 2021

Martin Svaneborg
AUTHOR

TRINITY

The *I*, *We*, and *They*
of communication

The lost secrets of public speaking,
and why we talk at all

Half a life's work by
Martin Svaneborg

"Don't eat the big white mint!"
- Sam Elliot

PROLOGUE

THE YOUNG MAN stood at the curb, looking across the street towards the stage door. He pulled up the collar of his coat. The icy wind bit his face as it hastened down the street. He looked at his hands. Trembling. It was not from the cold, though. Thoughts of confusion furiously hurled around in his head. *What does he want from me? I have given everything I have to give.* Tears were already swelling up behind his eyes. There was no world in which these next few hours would go well. Hesitantly, he walked across the street, pushed the handle of the stage door and disappeared into the darkness.

INTRODUCTION

**"The single biggest problem with communication
is the illusion that it has taken place."**
- *George Bernard Shaw.*

Why is this important? Trust me, it is. Very important. Do you need this book? Absolutely not. You will probably be fine without it. Is this a self-help book? No, and don't even get me started on self-help books, because they rarely work. A wisdom-book would be a stretch. This is an experience-book, and hopefully the read will entertain enough for you to stick around until you realise that you have learned some-thing precious along the way. Do I have something to offer? Yes. Without a shadow of a doubt, yes, I do. They say: *You learn from your mistakes*. I have failed so many times in my life that I have lost count many times over. So, if you want to learn how to fail in life, this is absolutely the right book for you. Of course, you could also be really clever and use it to learn how to avoid making the mistakes I have made. Let's go with that one.

Then, why have I written a book that undoubtedly will reside under the category of *self-help*? Well, I guess I have to stick this book somewhere, and the *autobiographical, philosophical wisdom by obnoxious, self-proclaimed preachers* category has yet to be introduced in books stores. It is not a biography or memoir per se. Too many wise remarks along the way. So, *self-help* it is – may God have mercy on my commercial soul. Hopefully, you will find the intent of the book is admirable, and that it is the concept of *self-help* itself, which has room for improvement. I don't remember who so brilliantly remarked that the concept of *self-help book* itself is contradictory. *Self-help* should mean you can help yourself, right? So, if you ask someone else, it is no longer *self-help* but just *help*. It should be called mere *help-books*. It just sounds a bit pathetic. Well, is this a help book then? No, because who am I to assume that you are weak and need my help?

This book is simply me pouring my heart out and spilling onto the page a life's worth of experience lived in half a lifetime. Sounds vague? I know, so let's make some decisions and get to the point. In this world, not only filled but overloaded with people spilling their guts in all sorts of forums, communication is growing increasingly difficult. Social media rules and governs how we communicate and interact. We have moved away from being social on media, to being narrowminded individualists, all hooked on getting the attention of everyone else. Whether it is social media or any kind of communication, we are getting sucked into a vortex of everyone, in their own little bubble, going *how do I get them to notice me? To like me. To respond with me.* But everyone else is busy thinking exactly the same. What is this book really about?

It is my goal with this book to show you that the noise of social media or your everyday life is not the problem. The content and information overload of our generation is not the enemy. We can't blame it on the flood of videos of cute cats and talking huskies. And the video of the mission impossible like squirrel climbing across a world of obstacles to get to the nuts… Have you seen that? Unbelievable! When and why do we choose to watch a video to the end? Can a video hold our attention for over 3 seconds? The answer is: Yes! Obviously. The cats, huskies, and Tom Cruise impersonating squirrels are solid proof. There are videos that we see to the end, because the content and message is somehow AMAZING. The video of the leader who denies science and a global pandemic only to get infected by said pandemic, oh, the irony… THAT we see... to the end. But the brilliant mind who goes on camera with an idea to cure Alzheimer's, or the unique young entrepreneurs, with a plan to build education for the global south, or the company trying to change the landscape of corporate values… 10 seconds, and we scroll on. WHY? Why does this kind of content not trigger us? Why does it not amaze us? The issue is not the content – the issue is how the message of the content communicates!

This is my promise to you. At the end of this book, you will know how you can create a message that will make people listen and care. If you do not put this book down feeling a responsibility to find your voice and with a sense of obligation to use your voice for something better than the hundreds of videos, you ignore every day as you scroll on down... Then I have failed.

Looking back on my life, every single problem I have encountered could have been solved or handled better, if I had been able to communicate in a way I could not. Everything we are in this world is defined by our ability to communicate. How we handle the job interview, how we do our job, how we talk to our loved ones and friends, how we talk to ourselves, and even how we identify ourselves is defined through our communication with those around us. The problem is, and it really is quite a problem, that communication is not getting any easier. We, as a human race, are really not making it easy for ourselves. We have created an abundance of applications, social platforms, etc. that make us turn away from communication. All the inventions should connect us, but separate us instead. We do not really talk to each other anymore. We state things. We say a lot of things, but we do not listen, and we do not ask questions with the purpose of understanding and learning, and THAT is a problem. To find an identity and a life of meaning and happiness, we need to be seen and be heard, but we cannot get through anymore. Our messages drown in the flood of content out there; a flood of near biblical proportions, but we will get back to the biblical part. We need to cut through the torrential storm of impressions, find our own voice, and take responsibility for using that voice for something better than the thousands of posts, messages and videos we ignore every day. All of them messages from people, who, just like you, are dying to be heard but are not because you and everyone else ignore them. This is my promise to you: At the end of this book, you will be inspired to find a voice of your own. At the end, you will know how to create a message that people will not ignore; a message that people will respond to. You will be seen. You will be heard. The clue is in the title.

Public speaking is THE greatest asset in your life. Period! Exclamation mark. There is nothing you can add to your life or business that will provide more power or value than public speaking and communication. If you can stand up in front of a crowd of people, and make them trust you, move them, and make them follow you, then you can achieve anything. Then you are on par with Jesus. Not bad, ey?

Everything I have learned so far in my half of a lifetime, I have distilled into a trinity of good content. It is an elusive paradox of personal value that goes into creating a message and communicating it in a way that make people connect with you. When your communication connects with other people, this is where the magic happens. This is where you find yourself and your true purpose. Wow, that just got deep at the end.

Disclaimer: I have both a stage background AND studied theology. Double trouble on the melodrama. Sorry. So, let me double down by using someone else's words. A young Kenyan photographer, Boniface Mwangi, who had witnessed the atrocities of political oppression in his country, wisely said: *There are two most important days in your life. The day you are born, and the day you discover why.* Whether he was the first to come up with that or not, I cannot say, but true it is.

While we are at it, though, let me make another disclaimer about my choice of words. Not my terrible humour in general or sorry excuses for sounding clever, but one word in particular. The *stage*. I have identified most of my life through having been a performer. A song and dance man. An actor. So, when I refer to *the stage* as in, when you decide to communicate, I do not mean literally taking to the stage. I assume the majority of all people have never stumbled onto a stage, unless they were really drunk, and the false premise of a karaoke party combined with the fourth dirty martini created a totally unplanned outcome. This book is not just for public speakers, politicians, and performers. When I refer to *taking to the stage,* I mean every time you summon up the guts to raise your voice and speak out to more than one person at a time; every time you stand up and claim the spotlight; every time you demand the attention by letting your voice be heard. You *take to the stage.* This shall be our lingo.

How to get the most out of this book. I highly recommend, while reading this book, to have a notepad close by. By the end of the book, I want you to have the outline for a speech that could end up being your signature speech. A lot of tips and tools will be given during Act 1 and 2, and I want you to turn it into your own ideas along the way. Act 3 is more philosophical, and by the end of the book you will hopefully feel inspired but may have forgotten many of the practical details. So, take notes and turn it into your own project.

Let's get started. First, a super quick overview. Here is the Trinity, as it will unfold.

1. Get skilled as a communicator. Otherwise, you will be misunderstood or just not taken seriously at all.
2. Dare to be honest and assume you will offend some, in the name of curiosity and understanding
3. Get your purpose straight. Make sure you communicate for the right reason.

Let's dive in. No, wait. One more thing. We need a framework and a narrative for this. Others have used the word Trinity before, on a much grander scale than this. Having studied both performing arts and theology in my life, why not take *Trinity* in the full, holy sense of the word and indulge ourselves completely in the awe-inspiring scope of this magnificent word? Let us take the actual Holy Trinity as the framework of our venture. THE Trinity, some might say.

The Father, the Son and the Holy Spirit. After all, this is the historical past of our western civilisation, for conveying not only the communication of culture and art but also conveying important messages to us, and that is what this book is all about; making sure you will say what needs to be said with the best possible outcome.

ACT 1

THE FATHER

1

THE REALLY GOOD STORY – PART 1

EVERY GOOD MESSAGE needs a good story, and the story in this book goes like this…

Once upon a time in a faraway land, where ugly ducklings turned into beautiful swans; where lives were understood backwards but lived forwards; where princes in ancient castles lamented over life and death; being or not being, while holding up skulls in wonder – yes, the above was a test of your knowledge about the country of Denmark (you can find the answers in the back of the book) – there lived a young man, whose wildest dreams were about to come true. Or so he had thought.

It was not many years ago that these dreams had been planted in his young mind. Like the mustard seed, the dreams had grown in good soil and taken a firm hold of him. Since his first appearance on stage in a high school play, the rush of adrenaline from the recognition of the applauding audience had taken him off guard. It was an instant craving for more. In only a few months, he went from the quiet kid in the class to the outgoing performer who sought every opportunity to get into the spotlight.

The kid grew into a young man. He studied his craft and became good. He had talent. He could go all the way. The sky was the limit. He was accepted into a leading academy for the Performing Arts, and five years later he was ready to make his professional debut in a musical. Most up-and-coming performers started out doing ensemble work for a few years, before they got a role. Not this young man. His first show was in a leading role. The role of The Emcee in the musical *Cabaret*. All the attention. All the spotlights. All the responsibility.

He was only nine hours away from the opening night. From what he expected to be his big breakthrough. He could envision all the raving reviews. All the comments and the praise that would come from both audiences, fellow cast members and, of course, family. The phone calls in the weeks to follow with offers about other roles. And maybe most important of all... The girls he could impress. The sex he would get. That all of this was not to happen, because he was not aware of other peoples´ general perception of him being rather arrogant, was a different matter. He had already envisioned it all, because he was that confident, and confidence is so easily mistaken for arrogance. Or at least he had been, because right now he could not feel his usual confidence. It had all but evaporated.

It was a week ago, since the entire cast had moved the production from the rehearsal space onto the main stage. Full orchestra in the pit, technical rehearsals, lights, sound check, costumes, wigs, make-up – everything being tied together. However, the director suddenly seemed to have changed his opinion about the young man and his rendition of the role. The young man had primarily worked with the American choreographer for the first four weeks of the rehearsal. The director had just seen some fragments of the performance until they were now going into the crucial and stressful phase of putting it all together. This is where things changed for the worse.

Every night, after each run-through of the show, the young man only got negative feedback that he did not know how to respond to. Feedback like:

"You are too nice. It has to be uglier. It is not enough."

The young man did not know how to be ugly. He did not want to be ugly. He wanted to dazzle the crowds. Every night he tried to up his game, but just got the same opaque feedback from the director. Finally, after the last dress rehearsal the director had proclaimed to the young man in front of the entire cast:

"Can you come in tomorrow morning for an extra rehearsal? I want to go over all of your solos."

The young man felt a torrent of emotions he was unaccustomed to and ill-equipped to deal with. He felt ashamed for getting bad reviews in front of the others. He felt confused, because he did not know how to deliver what the director wanted. He felt physically and emotionally drained for having rehearsed and performed his ass off for five weeks, seemingly in vain. He felt lost.

Of course, he was blissfully unaware of the fact that the problem had nothing to do with his performance or his talent or his efforts. The problem was the young man should never have been on a stage in the first place. Only much later would he discover that he was there for all the wrong reasons.

2

FATHER ISSUES

IF WE LOOK at the father represented in the Holy Trinity of Christianity, what is the father? Is he just God? And what the hell do I mean by *just*? Is he the creator? The one who has provided us humans with the skills we need to live in this world? What does the Father represent in the Trinity?

At first glance, the Father in Christianity, meaning God, seems to have been a pretty annoying father. One of those really pushy ones, who have to shove the son into all sorts of sports with the rotten argument that it will be good character building. *I'm going to send you to Egypt on government and housekeeping camp. It will help you find yourself. You will gain respect for yourself. I have signed you up for mountain bush burning. You need to learn to listen. You should try out for the desert solo wandering team. It will mature you and give you insight.* When you are the child in the middle of it, it can, at best, be mildly annoying and at worst traumatising. Then again, there is nothing that can keep you busy as an adult like a couple of good, wholesome childhood traumas.

To me, my father was just like the one in Christianity, the one who instilled a bunch of ideas in me. Mostly bad ideas, which he obviously thought were ingenious, as an alcoholic always views the world through the magnificence of his own genius. Ideas that caused me to make a truckload of mistakes. He caused an awful lot of trials and tribulations in my life, but eventually he was also the one whom I now owe the greatest debt of gratitude. Because of him, I am now a stronger, more complete person. A person not easily scared or offended. A person able to feel gratitude. Unfortunately, he never lived to see his awesome creation in a well-functioning version. Not in its entirety anyway. While he was still alive, he was always proud of me, but what he saw was a smokescreen hiding the truth about a broken young man. To me, my father represents the same as the father in the Holy Trinity does. He was even what I consider being the very definition of God; the version of ourselves we forever aspire to be. Of course, there is no way in hell, pun intended, that I aspire to become like my dad, or come to think of it, I do. When I so vehemently assume to reject the notion of becoming like him, it's because I never want to project my flaws onto others the way my dad did onto me. I don't want to be and never will be an alcoholic like him. I will never live a life in denial, clouded by booze, and refuse to own up to my mistakes the way he did. But I will be the proudest person on earth if I can get even close to the love he had for his son and the compassion for other people that lived in the depths of his tormented heart.

So, to even approach the first part of this trinity of good content I have laid out, getting skilled as a speaker, communicator or just as a human, we first have to look deep within ourselves. What creates us? What shapes and forms us into what we call ourselves, meaning our adult identity. Who is that person you see in the mirror, and who is that person you want to get skilled? How have you become all that you are; the good, the bad and the ugly? You can't expect to get skilled if you're not honest about exactly who that person in the mirror is, whom you now have to deal with in this process. I will go into more detail about this and how to bridge yourself; your personality with a sense of authenticity in a later chapter called *embrace the dark side*. And disclaimer (Yes, another one, and far from the last): In a process like this, should you choose to embark on it, it may very well prove to you, most unexpectedly, that everything you thought to had sorted out already about yourself, may prove unfinished business after all. The only thing you can count on for sure is: You did not create yourself. You don't have yourself to either thank or blame for who you are after the age of adolescence. You were created by someone else. You were created by nature, by the culture in which you have grown up, and hopefully by parents.

3

THE REALLY GOOD STORY – PART 2

THE YOUNG MAN tugged his coat tightly as he crossed the street and approached the stage door. The chilly rain slammed the door in waves. He pushed the handle resolutely to get inside and away from the cold. Once inside the darkness, he looked up the steep climb of stairs. He did not want to go up there. Everything in him wanted to run away. Run away from the confusion and the embarrassment. He felt so fragile. As if all it would take was the slightest poke and he would crumble into a heap of tears. The most frightening part of this state was the unknown. He had never felt like this. Fragile. Unsure of himself. At least not to the best of recollection. There was no way he could get on stage in this state. He knew it. There was nothing left to give. Knowing that this rehearsal was utterly pointless did not make matters any better. Opening night was nine hours away. He should be at the peak of his game right now. He should be feeling invincible. Instead, he felt like climbing these stairs was physically impossible.

Twenty minutes later he slumped down in a chair at the back of the grand auditorium facing the view, which the audiences would take in that same evening. The glorious view of the opening scene of their show. His show. His stage. But he saw nothing. He just sat there next to the lighting desk and the sound desk, with all the nobs and faders controlling the technique of the show, staring into his own hands with a dead look in his eyes.

Had someone walked by the young man, with a decent amount of empathetic acumen, they would have spotted the panic in the young man's eyes immediately. He searched desperately inside his untangled mind for answers to this bewildered state of his, but found nothing. No answers. No solution. No comfort, and no salvation. How was he to know that he was on the verge of a nervous breakdown?

Abruptly and late, the director burst through the side doors with papers and scripts falling out of his hands and exalted, "Alright, let's get started. You just get up on stage, and we'll take it from the top."

The young man uttered no words, but a river of tears started flowing down his face at a steady but seemingly relentless pace. He felt paralyzed from head to toe. Unable to stand. Unable to perform. The director was caught off guard and had not been aware of the young man's mental decline over the past week. Moments of awkwardness resembling an eternity of indecision passed before the director again took charge. He had likely pondered his options and had to priori- tise. What was more important to the director? The rehearsal and the changes he wanted in his leading character, or a functional actor for opening night. Eventually, there was of course only one outcome, as the young man was in no shape for rehearsal. The director dismissed him and left as abruptly as he had arrived.

The young man sat in the silent auditorium for a while, before he finally dragged his tired body out of the chair. For the first and only time that morning, he glanced into the silence of the empty theatre. It was strange how silence could seem to reverberate. Some technician had arrived and was fiddling around on stage. The young man buttoned up his coat, which he had not bothered to remove before the scheduled rehearsal, and left. With tears still streaming out of his eyes, he walked back down the stairs, out of the stage door in the back of the theatre, and down the street away from the street. He kept walking. Kept crying.

4

GIVE THANKS TO ARISTOTLE

THANKFULLY, when it comes to communicating, wise men have gone to great lengths to get skilled at this, for not only hundreds but thousands of years. And they came up with some pretty cool stuff even before that Jesus dude came onto the scene.

I said earlier that to work on the skills of being a better communicator, we first have to get honest with who we see in the mirror. As Michael Jackson famously phrased it: *I'm starting with the man in the mirror.* What a song! Anyway, side-step. We can lean with comfort and trust on the philosophical and rhetorical wit of Aristotle, in marrying the ideas of yourself with the skills of communication. If you think of Jesus as the beginning benchmark in time, when messages of great importance began circulating, then Aristotle beat the Nazarene to the punch, as Aristotle formulated the triad of rhetoric a good four-hundred-and-fifty years B.C. Or BCE (Before the common era) as is now the politically correct term, because god forbid, we should offend atheists and other religions with B.C. (before Christ), and changing it now, somehow makes the two-thousand years of labelling the most universal construct in the world, time, after one religion, much better. Yes, Aristotle created an awesome trinity that pre-dates even the almighty one.

He originally designed this triad or trinity with persuasive oratory in mind, meaning being able to convince an opponent of the validity of your argument. In my opinion though, and my opinion matters (because I am inherently valuable and thus awfully important. Cliffhanger), we can use the triad of rhetoric in an even cooler way that has an even greater impact on your life, your work, your relationships, and your ability to use your voice for good. Before I get to that, I have to first explain to you the triad of rhetoric in its original form, but also a little about Aristotle, because he was quite the dude.

The basic triad of rhetoric looks like this:

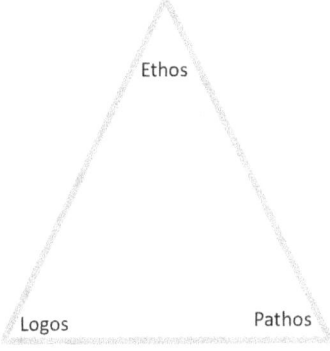

Ethos (Εθος) = Credibility
Pathos (Παθος) = Emotion
Logos (Λογος) = Logic/message

If you see this from a persuasive point of view which is used in politics, debates, et cetera, then the triad is used, as you apply the three points as different angles from which to reach the common goal in the middle being persuasion. It is a shitstorm of coming at the opponent from different angles, with different tactics for how to leave your assailant in the dust. But first, before we dive into the wonders of ethos, pathos and logos, as promised, we first have to get acquainted with Aristotle, so you understand where these strange words and concepts come from.

Let's just start by stating that he was awesome. Almost in the biblical sense of the word. I mean, how can you not assume Aristotle was awesome when he looked like this:

Okay, this depiction is probably somewhat enhanced regarding his physique. He likely didn't have that Avengers level muscle tone, given that he spent most of his days writing or traversing colonnades with fellow philosophers and students pondering the grander ideas in life. But other depictions of him conclude that he was in fact that much the man. Sixpack or not.

We know not all that much about Aristotle's life, which is not strange given we are talking a good two-and-a-half-thousand years ago. Documentation is limited. We do know that he was born in a lovely little city called Stagira, a good 50 kilometers east of modern-day Thessaloniki, Greece. Growing up, his father was the personal physician to King Amyntas of Macedonia, meaning a sure way to stellar living conditions and the finest of education. At the age of about 18, Aristotle moved to the sophisticated metropolis capitol of Greece, Athens, where he studied with none other than superstar philosopher, Plato. After becoming Plato's prodigy, we mostly know everything Aristotle wrote, but not all that much about what the man was up to, other than a quarrel over the legacy of Plato's academy, a stay at Lesbos, et cetera. However, the pivotal event we know is when Aristotle returned to the monarchy of Macedonia to become the personal tutor to the crown prince, Alexander, who went on to become not just any Alexander, but Alexander the Great. Yes, THE Alexander the Great, who later steamed through Asia Minor and Northern Africa to establish an empire, with the intended capital being the crown jewel of his achievements; the mythical town of Alexandria in Egypt, holding what was said to be the largest library in the world. Aristotle's ideas were spread far and wide.

What were those ideas? Well, they are most simply explained by setting them up against those of Plato, because the two dominant thinkers fundamentally disagreed. There is a famous fresco by Raffaello Santi (better known as Raphael) called *The School of Athens*, which depicts all the famous thinkers with Plato and Aristotle arguing in the middle. Plato points up to the sky to show his stance that all ideas we have come from a realm above, from whence they inhabit us, and to where they will return after we die. Aristotle counters by holding a steady flat hand downwards saying, "Nooo, Master Plato. The ideas are in this world with us. They are born out of our senses; what we see, hear and feel."

He kind of invented the concept of empirical experience about two-thousand years before David Hume made it a trend and pissed Immanuel Kant off to such an extent that he created a life's work of transcendental idealism, categorical imperatives, morality laws and all that jazz.

Amongst a lot of impressively deep philosophy, the time period and world view considered, Aristotle also wrote some very cool, down to earth, easily accessible stuff. He formulated some of the first writings on the now highly trendy topic of morals and ethics. Aristotle's Nicomachean Ethics are surprisingly simple, yet applicable even to today's society. For example, he described the *golden mean* or golden middle way, which is now a deeply embedded part of how we relate to each other, how we identify virtue, and what we now naturally consider good behaviour. The golden mean is the ever-present balance needed of all virtues to call them ethical virtues, and how others should perceive our virtues in order for said virtues to be of positive use to us. Example:

Aristotle's Golden Mean
Example: Courage/Confidence

Too much of it	Golden mean	Too little of it
Recklessness	Courage/Confidence	Cowardice
BAD	GOOD	BAD

A big part of his studies and the... well, philosophy of philosophy was not just the deep thoughts about the meaning of life, and where thoughts come from, but also applying it to living a more constructive, happy and fulfilled life. A lot of thought went into how to use the thinking to construct a better society. But let's leave Aristotle's philosophy. Since society rests on our ability to not only think but communicate, hence the invention of not only philosophy but rhetoric, and now we are finally back at the triad. Ethos, Pathos, Logos.

EXPLAINING THE TRIAD OF RHETORIC

Ethos = Credibility

Ethos comes from the Greek word, ἐθος, which means *custom* or *habit*, meaning *that which we do often*. And that which we tend to do often defines how others look at us and define us. Therefore, we now define *ethos* as *credibility*; the things about us that make other people listen to us, take us seriously, and eventually believe us. The reason this has to come first in communication, is that it is pointless to think about what to say or how we should say it, if we not first establish why on earth they should ever listen to us in the first place? Whatever you want to say, why are you the right person to say it? What gives you the authority and the credibility to talk about your particular chosen topic?

Pathos = Emotional connection

Pathos is the really fun one. This is the one where we get to go drama queen on the whole thing. The word, in ancient Greek, has a double meaning, but basically means *that which happens*. Very specific, right? That which happens is that which we experience, and that can have two meanings. 1) *When an incident befalls one* (We really should use *befall* more often. Love it) *creating an experience of suffering, misfortune or even calamity.* Dramatic much? 2) *An experience of the soul, experiencing a passion or emotion such as love or hate.* So basically, pathos is the drama in communication. Your emotional expression.

Logos = The message

Oh, my god, and pardon the pun, again. This is where it gets interesting. At its core, **Logos** simply means *word*. Of course, a word with that basic of a meaning will ultimately end up having an absolute avalanche of different sub-meanings and uses. Back in the day of Aristotle, they usually referred to logos as meaning *stating a fact* or *an argument*. In the discourse of rhetoric, it means *the thinking* or *reasoning* behind an argument, and it's the reasoning part that has made it be translated as *logic* in modern day rhetoric. However, it's also a contextually polysemic word, meaning it can have other meanings in other contexts. Allow me to deviate from our discourse for the briefest of moments.

———

Let's jump a few centuries down the timeline from Aristotle. You have seen this phrase before, right?

"In the beginning was the Word, and the Word was with God, and the Word was God."

This is the first verse of The Gospel of John from the bestselling book of all time called The Bible. Now, this gospel was originally written in Greek, where it looks like this:

Ἐν ἀρχῇ ἦν ὁ λόγος, καὶ ὁ λόγος ἦν πρὸς τὸν θεόν, καὶ θεὸς ἦν ὁ λόγος

Transcribed into the English alphabet it sounds like this, ish:
"En arxea en o logos, kai o logos en pros ton theon, Kai theos en o logos."

Bearing in mind that you now know what *word* is in Greek, do you recognise anything interesting? Yes, Logos (ὁ λόγος), The fourth word in the Greek text. (Ah, that is so funny because the fourth word is *word*. Ha!) What is really interesting is that in this context the word *word* does not really mean *word* at all. (I know it's confusing. Stay with me and keep your eyes on the prize). To paraphrase, the above verse means something along the lines of… Oh, and a super geeky note on the official translation, where the first part is translated: *In the beginning there was the word.* In the Greek original there is no definite article (*the* in English) in front of *beginning*, but there is in front of *word* (ὁ λόγος). So, the accurate translation is: *In a beginning there was the word.* Is that one little change from *a* to *the* not just mindbogglingly interesting? (Hint: think creation theory.) Anyway, a paraphrase of the whole verse would be:

In a beginning there was the personified agent of God's creation and world-government, the personification was with god, and the personification was God.

Don't you just love language? In other words, the *word* means 1) *Jesus,* as in *the personified agent of God on Earth, 2) God, and 3) the message of God delivered onto Earth.* How about that for an achievement of one little… word?

This deviation just to point out what power a message can hold and what status it can derive. When we now dive into the use of the trinity of rhetoric, in our context of communication, let us not underestimate the awesome power of the Ethos, the Pathos and the Logos.

Using the triad of rhetoric

Instead of using Aristotle's rhetoric as a triad of tactics from which to bombard the opponent with a persuasive attack, I like to use it as a linear progression towards making a lasting impact with your listener. Even the shortest and simplest of messages or communications can encompass all the three components. There is a natural order of rhetoric that you have to adhere to, if you want your listener to go along with and ultimately be impacted and moved by your message. For this reason, the order of the three components has to be 1) Ethos, 2) pathos, and 3) logos. We can also put an interrogative word next to each of them: 1) ethos/why? 2) pathos/how? and 3) logos/what? This means: 1) Why are you the right person to convey your message, and why should your counterpart trust you enough to listen? 2) How are you going to convey the message, so your listener will actually care enough to stick around to the end. And finally, 3) what are you really saying? You must approach your communication in this order, and if you keep reading, you will see why.

THE REALLY GOOD STORY – PART 3

CONFUSED AND SCARED, the young man walked away from the theatre, with no real care where he was heading. He just needed to get away, and part of what scared him was that he did not understand why he wanted to get away. *What the hell was happening? Why was he feeling like this? Why was he suddenly afraid to get onto that stage?* He had never been scared to go on stage. The stage had for years been his safe place. The place where he felt seen and where people recognised his talent. He kept walking. He kept crying.

The theatre was in a province city about three hours from the capitol where he lived. The theatre had thus afforded an apartment for him during the production period. He passed the apartment without even considering going up there. He did not want to face his roommate in this condition. He did not want to be seen weak and not in control of himself. He was after all the leading man in the show, and he needed to feel as such. He headed for the sea. A good twenty minutes later he had waves tumbling towards him. He stood for a moment looking out over the uninviting, rough winter sea, with all these conflicting thoughts and feelings swirling around in his head. The tears kept coming and kept icing up on his skin of his cheeks. He turned and walked along the water. He got the earplugs out of his pocket, put them in his ears and pressed play on the old cassette Walkman inside his pocket. He knew which tape was in. The same that had been playing an hour earlier on the way to the theatre.

Why was the director being like this? It was like he had suddenly decided he wanted someone else to play this part. Like he had just changed his mind about casting the young man in the first place. Like the director wanted to start over and redirect the entire character, with a week to go until opening mind. *Why doesn't he trust me? I have worked day and night for five weeks on this character. On this show. We were doing fine and now it's like everything I do is wrong. All that he says is: it's too nice. I have to be uglier. What does that mean? Well, tell me how! I can't redo the whole character now. What did he expect? And I don't want to be uglier.* The young man was years away from realising what was going on. The director had broken the young man's otherwise rock-solid confidence in himself. An hour later, the music in his ears stopped. He stopped and looked up from the rocky beach his eyes had been fixed on for his feet to navigate. The wind on his face made him aware that he had stopped crying. He glanced out over the relentless waters and finally came to a realisation. *I can't give him what he wants, because, apparently, what he doesn't want is me. All I can do is get on that stage tonight and enjoy myself. I'm just going to enjoy myself.*

A few hours later, the curtain went up. The warmth of the spotlight hit the young man's face. The orchestra set in, and he started to sing.

THE CRITERIA OF MAKING
SOMEONE LISTEN

TO MAKE ANYONE LISTEN, there are two criteria, which have to be met, before we can even get to the part of using the trinity and all our skills of communication.

CRITERION #1

Keep their attention and don't distract your listener

To draw on my own background as an actor, let's take to the actual stage. Imagine you're in a theatre. A great big, beautiful theatre with a chandelier in the ceiling, balconies, velvet seats, and the whole nine yards. The curtain goes up; the lights come on and the actors enter. You're ready, expecting to be taken in by what they have chosen to do on stage. You're ready to be moved, wowed, impressed, dazzled, provoked, humoured, and entertained. However, within the first five minutes one actor stumbles. Another forgets a line. This happens a few times within the first fifteen minutes. Will you be moved, wowed and impressed? No. You can't be moved, because you get distracted by their mistakes. You get distracted by the fact that they seem incompetent and unprepared. It seems like they don't quite know what they are doing up there. We can't follow them on that journey that should move us, because we're simply distracted. Because they distract us with their mistakes, they lose credibility in our eyes, and then we won't trust them enough to surrender to the emotional premise of the performance. The very first thing that has to happen, when you take to *the stage* (remember, I now mean when you speak to more than one person at a time), is that you have to earn the listener's trust. A trust, safe enough to get emotionally invested in your story. A trust only awarded because it seems like you know what you're doing; are competent at communicating, and knowledgeable about your message. The quickest way to fail at communication is to make sure that trust is never established in the first place, and the most efficient way to fail in gaining their trust is simply to distract them. You will be surprised how easy it is to distract your listener involuntarily and unconsciously. In fact, half of what you can come up with of brilliant ideas to enhance your mesmerising display of communication, could just as well backfire, and do just the opposite. Distract.

Examples of good intentions gone stupid distractions:

- You want to be more energetic and vivid in how you talk, so you talk really loudly, with a lot of expression. You are thinking: *I'm really engaging.* They are thinking: *Why are you talking so loudly? Feels fake*.
- You want to be concise in your appearance, so you deliberately narrow your body language down to a

foot apart-power-stance and arm/hand movements that only vary between the *holding the imaginary brick* hands and the *horizontal pyramid* hands. You are thinking: *I'm being super professional and executive looking.* They are thinking: *Why are you only doing those two weird figures with your hands? Is it sign language?*

- You want to use the space more, when you are standing up to speak, so you get the awesome idea of saying one point in one place on the stage (lingo reminder! Could be a boardroom). Then you take a few steps to the side, when you get to the next part of your message, and so on. You're thinking: *This is so clever. I'm linking physical areas on the floor with different points I'm making, thus making it easier for the listeners to stay with me and understand my points.* They're thinking: *Why are you walking sideways? You look like a crab!*

Enhancing the level of your communication is a very tricky and a subtle art that can't be packaged into *10 powerful tips to become a world-class speaker.* Because everything you could possibly think of to enhance the delivery of your communication, potentially has the risk of doing the exact opposite, if you end up not looking like a freaking human. All the skills in the toolbox are useless if you do not know how to use them while being able to maintain the appearance of a normal human being acting just like whoever is listening, whom we assume is also a human being. This is why everything starts with the ethos. It starts with establishing why you are credible and with earning their trust enough to surrender and go along with you on the journey towards your message. And at any point along the way, you can distract them, break the trust, and lose them.

CRITERION #2

Authenticity

To make people listen, be authentic. This sounds relatively simple both to understand and achieve, but oddly enough, it is often much more difficult to do, and much more difficult than you will accept it to be.

I can phrase the solution quite simply. To make others really listen, dare to look them in the eye while you talk. Literally. If you really pay attention to other people speaking or observe other peoples' conversations, you will see how few are truly comfortable with eye-contact. Unfortunately, we live in a world where face-to-face conversation is avoided, and, when undertaken, driven by an assumption of mutual judgment creating a hesitation and fear of being honest and authentic; of being yourself. The consequence of this is that most people avoid eye-contact. To quote the wonderful cinematic masterpiece, *Love Actually*: "It's a self-preservation thing, you see."

To put the solution slightly less simple, not that you have to have eye-contact per se to make people listen, but you have to be brave enough to look at your listeners to check if they are actually paying attention, and here is the rub: If you're not comfortable looking at them to check if they are looking at you, they're probably not. Thus, they are most likely not listening either.

The assumption of being judged for what we say causes the single biggest factor inhibiting people from either public speaking or just having and honest conversation, where you want to state your opinion. The single biggest factor is simply the fear. Fear of speaking. I will return to the fear of public speaking and the psychology, which both creates and maintains it, in a later chapter. Of course, you can skip to that chapter right now, if you, like so many others, suffer from this problem, but I MUST WARN YOU... if you do, you become a sinful, bad, BAD, reader for skipping ahead in the book, and not following the narrative chosen with diligence, care and love by the author.

To get back to the core of the second criterion of attention, authenticity, if you are not comfortable enough in your skin to get on stage, look your audience in the eye, and demand their attention, you will not come off as your own authentic self. If they do not see the authenticity of you, they will not perceive you as credible, they will not trust you and your voice, and ultimately you will lose their attention.

Can you regain the attention of your listener? Absolutely. BUT it requires the above and is a side bonus of being able to gain their attention in the first place. It is very easy to regain attention, actually. As you speak, if it is in front of a crowd, you let your eyes wander around the crowd to check if everyone is paying attention. If you spot someone who has clearly zoned out, here is what you do:

The Attention Trick

You strategically stop dead in your sentence at a random comma and look directly at the person not paying attention. After just a second or two, that person will be distracted out of their *not paying attention*, due to the sudden and unexpected silence. They will look right at you, momentarily confused, and as soon as they do, you continue your sentence, as if nothing had happened. To everyone else those two seconds of silence will look like you had a thought, because of the focused stare of yours. To you, it was a strategic pause to get that one person back on the band wagon. Works every time.

However, like with the above, it requires that you're confident up there in the first place to even expect their attention.

Now it's going to get a little deep. Because what does it take for you to get to where you are comfortable taking to the stage and raising your voice? But not only that, also expecting to be heard and acknowledged? What does it take for you to show the courage and vulnerability to show your own authentic self on stage? Well, I am sorry to potentially burst your bubble, but when you look in the mirror, you don't necessarily have to be content with what you see, but you do have to be at peace with what you see. And not only that, but every single memory and story from your past was a part of forming what you now see in the mirror. You must be able to revisit every memory and every story at any point in time and be at peace with them. Even the bad ones. *Really? Every single memory? Just to get up and speak? That seems excessive.* Here is why. You can't convey a message powerfully without linking it to your own personal stories and memories thereof. And if you can't revisit those memories and step into each one of them to share with someone else, being completely at peace with the memory, good or bad, then you will not come off as authentic.

Let me tell you a little story to prove this point. In a not-too-distant galaxy in a not-too-distant past, I had personally coached two people for an event where they were to give their very first ten-minute speech in front of a live audience. Stage, lights, microphone, crowd and all that jazz. Scarry stuff. But they were both well prepared. They had gone through the training and knew what they were doing up there. Their speeches were well crafted. The material was good. Strong messages. Well-staged to gain maximum use of the stage in their delivery. They both had speeches built on very personal stories. He spoke about discovering the endless sea of philosophy at an early age, leaving his native country and how to reconcile the loneliness of finding an identity in a big city with the potential suffocating vortex of philosophical thoughts pulling you in every conceivable direction; learning how to swim in the sea of life. She spoke about a troubled childhood with a conflicted relationship to a dominating sibling, learning how to choose to build a life and an identity for yourself, with the frightening prospect of having to take responsibility for your own actions, and no one to blame for the shortcomings of your life. Powerful stuff. By both of them. They both shared deeply personal stories on stage, which had had a profound impact on their respective lives. They were equally skilled and well-prepared up there. The only difference was that he was ready, psychologically, to revisit his own memories, step back in time and feel exactly what he felt at the time of the memory. She was not. She wanted to, and she knew even that it would be necessary to do so. But she couldn't.

The interesting thing is that before either of them got on stage, I personally think neither of them knew that one was emotionally ready, and one was not. Everything she thought she had reconciled with in her past was still unfinished. She was at a point where she had become functional with her past, but she was not truly at peace with it.

Before the event, I had taught both of them about the fear of losing emotional control on stage, and how the fear of embarrassment, by losing control of said emotions, can hold speakers back from being honest and authentic. I had also taught them how to deal with it, if it happened. So, when she took to the stage, she delivered a flawless speech. There was nothing wrong. It lacked the pathos of honest personal commitment to the story, but she got the applause she rightfully deserved as a skilled, well prepared speaker. When he took to the stage, there was an immediate presence between him and the audience. They felt him. They felt his past, his struggle and his desire to share the most difficult parts of him. They saw the images in their minds of his lonely, square room in London, and when he came to the most emotional part of his story, describing how he literally felt like drowning in confusion and suffering, internally, he, as a speaker, found himself standing at the edge of emotional control, staring into the abyss. He could have pulled back, gone into self-preservation mode, but he didn't. He jumped. He broke, and he cried. Weeping and stumbling over words, he fumbled his way through the rest of his speech, word by word, sentence by sentence. By the time his speech actually described him finding his way to safe shores and peace in his own life, so too did he regain control of his emotions and of his speech. As he closed and delivered the last sentence of his speech, his eyes were shiny with vulnerability. The crowd did not applaud. They erupted, and as he walked off stage, the tears still flowed from his eyes.

After the event, I asked both of them, individually, how they felt after the speech. She was all too aware that she had failed to go to the emotional place. She was proud of what she had achieved, as just a month earlier, she would never have dreamed, she could ever get up there at all. But she was also disappointed that she could not go where she wanted to go in the story and knew there was still work to be done. A week later, she had booked the first appointment with a psychologist. I asked him how it felt to lose control the way he did, and to experience being able to get to the other side, recover and finish the job. He said it was the most amazing thing he had ever experienced. That simple. That beautiful.

A few weeks later, I spoke to her again, and she asked me: How do YOU feel when you are up there speaking about something personal? I told her; it's not about wanting to or trying to be emotional up there. Sometimes you tell happy stories. Sometimes you tell sad stories. Sometimes you're all business. It's never an aim with a sad or deeply personal message or story to cry. In most situations, if you get up to speak, it will be considered unprofessional if you lose control and cry. But If you do, they will never hate you for it, because it's human to lose control. But you're not up there to cry. You're up there to speak. When I go on stage, this is what I do:

'I don't care!

I don't try to cry, but I don't care if I do. I don't try to laugh, but I don't care if I do. I am completely at peace with whatever emotion comes out of me, and I am at peace with showing it to strangers. Even if I should lose control up there, they won't hate me for it, and even on the off chance that my emotions should annoy them to the point where they walk out, I can live with that."

Without authenticity, without daring to go to the emotional side of yourself, you might appear skilled as a speaker, but you will not appear trustworthy. If that happens as a speaker, then I am sorry: Game over! So, before you get up there on that stage, take a long hard look at yourself in the mirror and ask yourself if you're really comfortable with what you see. Good or bad. If you're not, then you need to fix that first. Get comfortable with yourself. YES... I know, if you thought you could just take a 3-day crash course in public speaking and then nail every job interview, work presentation, wedding speech and break-up conversation, only to realise that you need something else that will require a few years of therapy, it may frustrate, but you will thank yourself later. Because, for your sake, that needed to be done, anyway.

7

THE REALLY GOOD STORY – PART 4

IN THE INTERMISSION after the first act, the young man sat in his dressing looking into the mirror in front of him. He was happy. There was a buzz in the air. Makeup artists, hairdressers and wardrobe were bustling around him, getting him ready for the second act. Five more numbers and five more costume changes. Suddenly, the American choreographer popped his head in and said, "I don't know what you're doing, but it's fantastic. Keep it up."

Then he was gone. The young man looked in the mirror and smiled.

The next day the reviews were in the papers, and they were good. Very good. The whole show got outstanding reviews as a well-crafted, highly entertaining and thought-provoking performance. The young man got special attention in numerous reviews, and one paper went so far as to crown him as *the shining star of the show*. Not a word from the director. Not a single word.

Ten years later, the young man had gone out of his usual private comfort zone to attend the birthday party of a famous vocal coach in the industry. He was not so young anymore and was supposed to be a grown up by now. He knew the place would be filled with like-minded peers from showbiz. All people that he actually did not care too much for being around, but he understood the importance of networking. This was such a day.

While hovering over the buffet pondering the difference between pawn and shrimp, as one does, a blast from the past was suddenly next to him. The director was there. The two had not spoken since the last performance of *Cabaret* ten years earlier. A new production of the same show was running at the time of the birthday party, so the young man found a way to ask some questions he had been yearning to ask for years.

"Have you seen the new *Cabaret*?"

"Yes. As a matter of fact, I have."

"What did you think of it?"

"It was good. I think ours was better."

The young man (and let us keep calling him *the young man*, for the sake of narrative consistency) snug a curious glance at the director to read his eyes to interpret the some-what vague statement.

"And what did you think of the *Emcee*?"

The director turned to the young man and looked him straight in the eye.

"Look. You have to understand. When we did the *Cabaret* together, it was personal to me. First, what you probably don't know is, I had already directed two produc-tions of *Cabaret* before the one with you. You are not the first Emcee I have directed. Second, I am German. Third, I am Jewish."

The young man looked at the director with a sudden empathy, as he knew what that meant. *Cabaret* was about an impossible love story in pre-second world war Berlin; a story about the holocaust and racism. The young man's train of thoughts had just left the station at full throttle, but the director stopped him dead in his tracks.

"Do you remember that day at rehearsal, when you sang your solo number, *I Don't Care Much* for the first time on stage? You tried to get out of singing it in front of the cast, sitting in the auditorium, because you were vain, but I forced you to do it, anyway. Just you and the piano. I have never heard anything like it. The whole auditorium fell silent, when you sang. You could hear a pin drop."

The young man looked up in surprise, but the director continued.

"I have never seen a better *Emcee* before or after you."

The young man was taken back. This was not at all the conversation or the response he had expected, and the impact and perspective of the director's words did not sink until he had left the party, and to a certain extent until years later.

Ten years earlier, the young man had been in the middle of his life's greatest opportunity to shine and become the star he so yearned to be. The director was dealing with a third go at a terrifying story about one of the darkest moments in human history, the holocaust, with a deep personal and cultural attachment to said history. And there the young man had been. A 25-year-old white kid playing the director's leading role, without a shred of a chance at understanding or grasping the enormity of the perspective the director had on the story. The young man had spent a solid five weeks of rehearsals trying to impress everybody and doing a fine job of it with everyone except the director, who did not care for being impressed. The young man had done exactly what all 25-year-old guys do. Try to impress. Because, at the end of the day, this is all guys care about at that age. Looking cool, so they can ultimately get laid.

However, that night, on opening night, for the first time,

the young man had walked on stage broken. He had lost the ability to impress. For a week, the director had disregarded his attempts to impress to where the young man had lost confidence in his confidence. The young man was used to walking on stage being vulnerable, with the courage that that requires. And actually, vulnerability does not require that much courage, but it will make you stronger. When the young man had a packed auditorium of people in front of him, he could easily accept that not all would like would he did up there. But he knew that if he did well, he could win most of them over to where the ones that did like him would be the majority. But for a week, his entire audience had consisted of one person only. The director. And when you have to go up there and you know your entire audience of one will disapprove of you; when you know you are going up there to be criticised, to be crucified... that is not vulnerability. That is psychological torture, which will not make you stronger. It will break you.

Suddenly, and for the first time, the young man was up there not trying to impress. He went up there with nothing but himself, whatever that was. That opening night was undoubtedly not his finest moment, but through that cracked armour shone the light of the artist inside the young man, and with the armour broken, that light continued to shine and grow brighter. Ultimately, the artist emerged. The artist, the director had wanted all along. Not necessarily an artist who had to be ugly, but an artist who dared to be honest.

8

THE CHARISMA PATTERN/
CREATING RAPPORT

I WANT to take a moment and distinguish between two fundamental forms of communication and some aspects and tools, which apply heavily to both of the two forms. And by communication, in this book at least, I hope you have gathered by now; I mean oral communication. The spoken word; you, using your voice.

Fundamentally, you can divide all forms of oral communication into either public speaking or private speaking, and define that as whether you speak to a crowd of people and having prepared to do so, or just to one person. Are you speaking or having a conversation?

When we as humans do either of the two, certain behaviours come into play driven by our deeply embedded settings for how to interact with each other as humans. It is long since scientifically proven that we all, statistically, like people who are either like ourselves or how we want to be. The wording is not even mine. Tony Robbins coined that one. Those people immediately attract us, and those people we will automatically want to listen to. Let me say that again, just because it's important, and the basis of everything in this chapter.

"We like people, who are either like ourselves, or how we want to be."

- Tony Robbins

The most powerful way to make someone listen, whom you want to convey a message to, is to appear as if you are like them, or someone they strive to be. Then they will automatically take you seriously, because they connect with you on a personal level. This phenomenon is called *rapport*.

There are several ways you can strategically build rapport with someone you communicate with. If it's over a one-on-one conversation, you can do simple things like mirroring the body language of the other person. Sit back and relax if they do. Take a sip of water if they do. Mimic the cadence and tone of their voice. Speak softly if they speak softly. Within minutes the person in front of you will feel connected to you thinking: *Wow, I really like this person. I feel like they get me.* When what's actually happening is, they're having an experience of *this person is just like me.*

If you're speaking in front of a crowd of people, then the Charisma Pattern also known as the V-A-K range comes into play. Overall, people can be divided into three boxes of personality. There are other systems with greater gradation and development of these personality traits. However, for speaking, I like the simplicity of this one. This is not meant in the psychological sense of personality, where there are far more boxes and parameters, and at least five big ones. This is meant as what kind of charisma you emanate to other people, and what kind of charisma you are attracted to. As we have already established that we like people who are like ourselves, we also like people who communicate like ourselves. Generally, we can divide our different types of charisma into three groups:

- V: Visual People
- A: Auditory People
- K: Kineasthetic people

Let me describe the three categories with the widest of stereotypical brushes, and I have used the following many times, both as an actor and speaker. Works like a charm.

Visual are the very energetic people. The ones who tend to be the centre of attention at parties, simply because their visual, vivid body language and animated, often loud voices automatically demands everyone's attention. They have big arm-gestures and epic stories of great impact and radical change, which means their mode of communication relies mainly on their own visuality. Tony Robbins is a prime example of a visual speaker. If you don't know him, go hide your head and the sandy dunes of shame for a day or two. And you know where to go after that.

Auditory are people who tend to go into politics. They're driven by sound. The voice. They like to talk, debate and persuade. They have speaking voices that are more or less in one place, but with great articulation and clarity. These are speakers like Martin Luther King, Jr. Not a lot of body language. Also, not a lot of emotion, but a lot of auditory power. *I have a dream that one day this nation will rise up and live out the true meaning of its creed: 'We hold these truths to be self-evident, that all men are created equal.'* This is a prime example of an auditory communicator using nothing but the authority and skills of his voice and the power of the words.

Kinaesthetic people are the sensitive ones. The soft ones.

They speak with careful voices and without body language. They need to listen and feel first. They need to be heard, understood, and even have their soul gently caressed before following along. They're the kind of people who become therapists or healers or life-coaches. Ironically enough, Tony Robbins, having more or less invented *life-coaching*, is the least kineasthetic person on the planet. There are exceptions to any rule. I always think of Ross from *Friends*, when I think of kinaesthetic people. Whenever Rachel opens the door, and on the other side is a subdued, emotionally timid Ross saying: "*Hi...*"

When we speak to others we will naturally speak, falling into whatever group we belong to as a person. If you are a visual person, you will speak visually. However, because we have already established that we like people, whom are either like ourselves, or how we want to be, we also prefer to listen to people belonging to the same group as us. Visual people will instinctively connect with other visual people, and thus more prone to listen to a visual speaker, and so on and so forth.

Because the range from the most highly energetic of visuals to the most sensitive of kinesthetics is so vast, the two can literally repel each other. The visual person will soon become frustrated and utterly bored with a kinaesthetic speaker, and the kinaesthetic will become intimidated and potentially even scared by the visual speaker, to the point of wanting to run away.

If you're in a one-on-one conversation, this is not necessarily a big issue. However, if a visual person is in a conversation with a kinaesthetic person, and none are aware of what they are, it will not be a lengthy conversation, and both sides will quickly find excuses to end the conversation., head for the hills or go search for your own tribe.

BUT if you're in front of a crowd, maybe even on a stage,

god forbid, neither you nor the crowd can just walk away. Sometimes the crowd can, and sometimes they will, which is an awful feeling to the speaker on stage. So, we must find common ground, and it's not the crowd's responsibility to do so. It's your responsibility. You, the communicator.

You have to create broad spectrum appeal, and this is where the awesome Charisma Pattern comes into play. And I almost do mean awesome in the biblical sense of the word, as it is awe-inspiring what you can achieve with it; the togetherness and trust you can create between people.

It goes without saying, if you're in front of a crowd of people, and unless it's your own seminar, where you have hand-picked the attendees based on pre-sign up questionnaires about personality types, or you have a 40-year career and brand behind you, and thus only attract the same kind of customers as yourself, then any crowd will comprise a multitude of personalities covering the entire V-A-K range. *Wow, that was a long sentence.* So, how do you get all of them to listen, when you're only one type yourself? Answer: **The Charisma Pattern!**

What you do is incorporate all the three types during your speech. Not all at once, but in a successive curve resulting in you having gained everyone's attention by the end. Who should we get on board first? The visuals? No. As described before in the conversation, highly visual people are merely bored and maybe annoyed and frustrated at most by the very kinaesthetic speaker. A very kinaesthetic listener, however, will be intimidated, and maybe even downright scared of the visual speaker to where they will physically leave the room. So, you start by getting the kinaesthetic people on board. The visual ones won't mind. Which means, you may need to do an opening sentence visually, just so everyone sits up in the chair and notices that you have started, but then you have to communicate with the kinaesthetic people. Speak to their soft sides; to their emotions and their need to be heard and understood. Tell them why you understand their hesitation at what is about to happen. Ensure them it is safe to go on this journey with you, and that it will be worth the patience and trust in the end. After a few minutes of that, you can move on to the auditory people. You can raise your voice, tell your story with clarity, authority and compassion. While you do this, the visual people will wake up from their slumber of boredom, and get interested, because authority and assertiveness speaks to them. When you finally go full blown visual for the grand finale, driving home the awesome message, everyone will love you. The visuals will love you, because you are smack in the middle of their world. The auditory people will love you, because you gave them what they wanted, and you are now still an enhanced version of them. Finally, the kinesthetics will still love you, because you started with them for once. They will be thankful and appreciate you for taking the time to get to know them and understand their perspective, and as a reward they will gladly stay with you until the end. This is the awesome power of the charisma pattern.

The Charisma Pattern
(within Aristotle's triad of rhetoric)

Ethos
Start kinesthetic (answer their "why?")

Pathos
Go auditory (Tell your story. Connect emotionally)

Logos
End visually (use your entire range
to deliver the message)

9

WHAT WE LEARNED FROM THE
REALLY GOOD STORY

OF COURSE, you are clever enough to have figured out that the young man in the really good story was me. What did I learn from having a nervous breakdown nine hours before opening night? I learned several things, and I kept learning from that experience for years to come.

First, it took me ten years to get to the conversation that could have solved my problem in the first place. I was getting worn down that week of rehearsals, because I didn't dare ask the director a single question back. In my youthful ignorance, I insisted on trying to win him over by just doing better. Trying harder. Trying to impress him when he had no interest in being impressed. The first lesson here, which I have used many times since, is this:

If you find yourself stagnating in your development, not getting anywhere, and there are people around you seemingly frustrated, because you do not meet their expectations, then trying harder is rarely the answer. Do not try and do better,

*do something differently instead. Change **how** you do things
and not how **well** you do things.*

Second, our human body is an amazing adaptation mechanism. It will always refer to a default setting if possible. As soon as you have done anything a number of times in more or less the same way, then you will struggle to do the same better, as the body will try to revert to the default setting you have created for protection. So, you stagnate. The way to develop is to break the default setting by doing whatever you do differently. My director did not want more of the same; a better version of what I already did. He wanted something else. Change, and you will develop. I have learned how to achieve development by asking the right questions. If I had had the guts to ask him why he was suddenly so displeased with my performance, I might have been able to understand what he wanted. I might have been able to avoid a very uncomfortable breakdown. Not that I wish that avoided, because I am very grateful today for that experience and what it taught me. Maybe I was afraid to ask questions, because I was so hung up on being good, and thus not wanting the answer to my question being that I was not. However, the answer would never be that I was not good enough. Of course, I was good enough. Otherwise, the director would never have hired me. Yes, the director might very well have got annoyed if I had asked questions about his reasoning, but here is the thing:

It is always okay to ask questions, even with the risk of offending someone, if the motivation is a desire to understand someone's perspective.

Third, I would not have become the artist I became, had it not been for that director. For five weeks I had gone through the rehearsal period, with a juvenile attitude of wanting to impress. Granted, the director was being a bit of a dick with his mode of communication. Just complaining about me, without giving me any concrete directions to work with, was frustrating and fruitless for the objective of opening night. But for me, in the long run, it forced me to shed my armour of fake confidence. When the armour broke, a man appeared from behind the armour. Not necessarily a well-functioning man. In fact, far from it, (let's return to that later), but a man who could become an artist. On opening night, I was still far from an artist; far from my full potential, but just the fact that I went on stage without the confidence, emotionally naked and honest, was far more interesting than anything I had done before. I am sure I was not as good as the director ten years later so kindly claimed me to be, but from opening night and every night from then on, I went on stage adding a little more to the artist. Suddenly that young man could develop, because the armour had been broken. A radical change had been made and development was inevitable to the point where, at the LAST performance of Cabaret, I was finally the Emcee he wanted all along. So, here is the final point of this story, so far:

Wanting to understand is a choice; a choice to recognise someone's perspective.

I'm forever grateful to the director for breaking me down. It's one of the greatest gifts I've received in my life. It not only launched a development towards my full potential as an artist, but, more importantly, because at the end of the day theatre is just theatre, it put me on a trajectory towards me ultimately becoming a better person, than I otherwise would have been. I still had years of mistakes, trials and errors ahead of me, but this moment was one of those moments that just kept giving. It has also provided me with an empathy for the director, because I now understand his perspective. I know why he was so frustrated, and not a day goes by where I don't wish I could do that role again. Just to give him what I now know he wanted, and that I now know I could do. I could do well.

ACT 2

THE SON

10

THE PATHOS OF JESUS

YEARS AGO, a child was born, who grew up to become quite special. We know little from his upbringing, but as a man, he became known as Jesus of Nazareth. The Nazarene from the region of Galilee. The man's message elevated him to a status, where he would become arguably the most famous person of all time. Jesus Christ, the Son of God. Quite the career advancement. A lot has been written about him in religious contexts, but because almost everything written about him is written with a religious motivation, it's fair to be skeptical about the legitimacy of those stories. Because of this fair skepticism, many even argued that the Nazarene didn't exist at all but was a figment of spiritual imagination crafted to derive power to a corrupt patriarchal institution in the making. However, most respected theological scholars now agree that the historical Jesus did exist. There is documentation (very little, but enough) describing Jesus in contexts where there would be no religious motivation for even mentioning his existence.

In the year 64AD, the roman historian Tacitus wrote this:

> *"Nero fastened the guilt ... on a class hated for their abominations, called Christians by the populace. Christus, from whom the name had its origin, suffered the extreme penalty during the reign of Tiberius at the hands of ... Pontius Pilatus,"*

Being a roman, Tacitus would have no personal or strategic reason to mention Jesus or what happened to him, as Rome at that time was not yet Christian. Similarly, the first-century historian, Josephus, mentioned not only Jesus but also his brother James, when he wrote this:

> *"… one James described by the Jewish Sanhedrin, the brother of Jesus the so-called Christ."*

The interesting thing here is obviously not the documentation of the existence of Jesus, but the question: Were you aware Jesus had a brother? Of course, he did. He had several. This was two thousand years ago. As opposed to our time, only children were very rare. But then again, he went on to become the one Son of God. So, I guess the misunderstanding is fair.

But if Jesus of Nazareth has had such a profound impact on our western civilisation, surely, we must know more about him, then just two or three trustworthy mentions in the 1st century Reader's Digest, Roman empire edition. So, how much do we presume to know about him? In the 19th century there was a whole surge of research, very Indiana Jones-esquely referred to as *The Quest for the historical Jesus*, done into uncovering and differentiating the historical Jesus from the divine one, the Christ, from which information (the bible and other religious documents) was considered convoluted and historically unreliable.

There are only a handful of things we can regard facts about the historical Jesus. He was obviously not Christian, since he did not become Christ until after his death and subsequently promoted resurrection. Jesus was a Jew, and he promoted a messianic version of Judaism to other Jews. This was not at all unusual at the time. There were hordes of groups popping up all over the place, with their own trending version of the coming Messiah. If you have ever seen Monty Python's *The Life Of Brian*, and remember the scene where the group sitting on the bleachers (like taken out of the sports arena of any American teenage musical movie), watching the gladiator fight, while arguing with Brian whether they are *The Judean People's Front* or *The People's Front of Judea*, you have no idea how on the nose that scene, and the whole movie is, to the historical situation in the region around the time when Jesus walked the holy land. The Monty Python guys had seriously done their homework.

We can also with a fair amount of certainty say that he had a mentor in formulating this messianic movement in the midst of the whirlpool of Jewish movements, and the mentor went by the name of Ἰωάννης ὁ βαπτίζων (John, The Baptist).

Finally, we know, for sure, that Jesus of Nazareth, as a result of his preaching this new kingdom of God on Earth, was accused of sedition, trialled and sentenced to death by crucifixion by the Roman empire. An all-powerful, totalitarian regime at the time of Jesus' birth ruled by Emperor Octavian, and at the time of crucifixion by Emperor Tiberius, governed in Jerusalem by Pontius Pilate. Oh yes, and we know he had at least one brother. That's it!

But then comes the inevitable and oh, so exciting speculation, because who are we, as humans, with our all to imaginary minds, to stop there, when the man turns out to be the freaking Christ? Let's start with why he got crucified, and that's actually not speculation yet, because this has a logical explanation seen through the lens of that time and place being the Roman empire. It's uncertain whether Jesus proclaimed himself to be the Messiah of this coming kingdom that he preached, but it is obvious to assume he did, given the tragic outcome of death by nails and starvation on a cross. Stating, at that time, that you were the Messiah meant you claimed to be the direct descendant of King David (*Messiah* literally means *the anointed one which was the initiation ritual of kings*), and thus have arrived to reunite the twelve tribes and usher in the final Kingdom of Israel. However, in the Roman empire there was a special clause in the emperor contract saying: When you become emperor, then you, by definition, also become a roman god. And we complain about CEOs getting lavish bonuses and lucrative retirement plans. The Romans took contractual benefits to a whole other level. By claiming to be the Messiah, the King and heir to the kingdom of the ONE true God, you also said that the emperor, on the other hand, was NOT god or the ruler of the world. And obviously the Emperor could not have people running around spreading that kind of nonsense. Also, the sentence of crucifixion was reserved exclusively for crimes against the state. Nails it was.

Semi-speculative, but for very good reason is the issue of his family. There is mention of four brothers of Jesus, the famous one of them being James (Jakob). Actually, we know much more about James, historically, then about Jesus. Much was written about James, who led the Jesus movement for about 30 years, which Jesus himself only led for three-four years. Now, how many brothers and sisters he had is obviously not the most exciting part of the family-issue. The speculation always skyrockets into a stratosphere of blockbuster producing books and movies by the one intriguing thought: Was Jesus married? The natural and highly logical response given the time and society in which he lived was, YES! Of course, he was married. A 30-year-old man, having a normal functioning life and a place in society at that time, not being married would be unthinkable. The only adult men living an unmarried life of celibacy were monks living within ascetic, monastic orders closed off from society. Jesus was clearly not closed off from society. On the contrary. He was actively taking part in society, trying to shape it for a better future. The huge conundrum is the fact that despite this logical assumption, not one piece of written documentation mentions marriage or a wife of Jesus. In various gnostic gospels there are vague hints at a personal relationship with Mary Magdalene, but out of the gazillion ancient fragments in existence, not once is there a concrete mention of a wife or a marriage. This is so conspiracy theory provoking it is almost irresistible.

The speculation could and have gone on forever, so far, but out of the meagre facts we have about this man, one awe-inspiring conclusion remains: Regardless what he was or what he was not, one thing is for sure. He must have been an incredibly inspiring person. He must have been one hell of an interesting dude to be around. Only a hundred years later, he was hailed as Christ, the Son of God, and two-thousand years later he is, to this day, still the most famous and written about person on the face of our planet. You do not create that level of attraction or end up with that kind of following without mad communication skills. He must have been a public speaker, second only to divinity. He must have been able to tell a story that would keep the listeners spellbound. He must have had a heart and a compassion for the people around him, that would make them follow him to the end of the world.

Jesus was the son, but also the messenger; the one going out in public; up on the stage to deliver the message. He was the one who had to be personal and authentic to gain the trust of the disciples.

In the light of the context of this book, it's interesting to ask what part Jesus played not only in the new testament but also in the later defined Holy Trinity. What was his role in the delivery of the message? Was he the ethos, the pathos, or the logos? Well, he was not ethos, because the identity of the message itself was God. God was the author and the credibility behind the message. He was also not the logos, although John (the apostle) would phrase him as such in his testament, because the logos from Aristotle's perspective was the message of God. Jesus was the pathos. He was the emotional connection between the credibility of the message and the recipients of the message. The listeners. The audience. Jesus was the narrative, the really good story of great virtue, making his followers as well as readers of the scriptures for years to come, want to listen to him, because they emotionally got invested in him. He told the stories, toured from village to village, did the good deeds and met the people in person. He was the one they looked in the eye. He was the one they chose to trust, and this is the power of the personal story and the pathos of rhetoric.

It's not a coincidence that the bible has become the best-selling book of all time, and not only selling above and beyond, but as of the year 2015, making over 2,4 billion people worldwide choose to believe the message conveyed by this book. Why? Because it's a really good story told really well and with great pathos. And if you're not happy with my argument of Jesus being a really good story, just from the book sales and the fact that you recognise his name, the reason it's such a good story is because the story of Jesus dying on the cross is the most fundamental of archetypal stories told in the history of myth and literature. The man getting punished in the most humiliating of ways, for having the best possible virtues, and preaching nothing but love and kindness. There is nothing more unfair and heart-wrenching than that, which is why it is such a commercial success. It has broad-spectrum appeal. A modern-day story with equal commercial success is that of Harry Potter. The orphaned, extraordinary wonder-child, living with ordinary muggle stepparents, whom praise their own muggle son, Dudley, for being an arrogant little brat, but punishes Harry for his virtues. So, Harry must go off in search of a place where his extraordinary virtues are acknowledged and appreciated. Punished for being kind. Same story. Same success.

11

PERSONALITY – EMBRACE THE DARK SIDE

EARLIER, I said that you have to know who it is you see in the mirror, and whether you are ready to take that person on stage in front of other people. Every time I went on stage, it was almost with a Jekyll & Hyde-type dual personality. It was like the flick of a switch, when the curtain went up and the lights came on. A person who I usually was not appeared and took over. A person I was not conscious of who was or where came from.

Psychologist, Carl Jung spent a lot of time studying this phenomenon, and he described it as your "shadow". The person you, unconsciously, give other people the impression of being in order to impress them. The persona you pretend to be. FYI, isn't it interesting that *persona* from Latin means *character* or *mask*? There are parts of your personality you're willing to face and own up to, but there are also sides of your personality, you're not willing to own up to. Those least desirable aspects of your personality, which you're not too keen on putting on display. They remain hidden in your unconsciousness, just outside the light of your everyday consciousness, until you reach a point in your life, where you become ready to face your own darkness. Your demons. The skeletons in your closet. They're called many things. You choose. It's your darkness.

> "Everyone has a shadow, and the less it is embodied in the individual's conscious life, the blacker and denser it is." - *Carl Jung*

That it is called a *shadow* and described by Jung as *blacker,* the less aware of it you are, does not mean that everything in your shadow is negative. It just means that the shadow becomes so black and dense that you can become all but blind to what is in there. For people with anxiety issues, or people who think very little of themselves, it can also be positive things in their shadow, which they unconsciously suppress to support the false idea of their negative self-image.

When I went on stage, it was my unconscious shadow that took over and showed the world the part of me, I wanted them to see. I tried to impress them, because the truth was, I was too scared to show them the real me. I was too scared to show that I was not okay. I was a scarred youngster with unresolved childhood issues, who needed attention, so I had built a nice little alter-ego, which flourished on stage. This was also why, unlike so many others, I never suffered from stage-fright. Quite the contrary. The stage was my safe place. My place of escape. The place where I didn't have to be me and could just be whatever the stage required me to be. I could be awesome and cool and totally in control of my life. That is, until a director, quite ruthlessly, got me to realise that that was not working out so well for me either. Eventually, I had to face my shadow. I had to embrace the dark side of me, and yes, I used those words to draw your attention to associate with Star Wars. Because how well was Luke Skywalker doing until he found out that his father was Darth Vader? Not so well. He could never reach his full potential and learn to harness the full power of the force, until he embraced the fact that he was the son of Darth Vader, and the dark side was a part of him too. Only then could he become a whole person. This is also why these types of stories work so well. They're archetypal stories that go deep into all of us and hits us at the core of who we are as humans and how we function, whether we want to admit it. If you can embrace your shadow, and take that on stage with you, not as an excuse or a replacement for the real you, but a part of you, then you hold the power. Then the force is strong in you.

Before you take to the stage to do your speech, look in the mirror and look closely. Are you sure you want to take all that up there? If you do, you could be amazing up there. You could change lives up there. If you're not willing to take everything you see in the mirror up there, that's fine too. But know that your speech will never be more than mediocre, no matter how many tricks and tools you learn. All the steps to the left, all the vocal variety, all the pauses, all the sandwich structure, all the tricks in the book will make you a fantastically mediocre speaker. Because if you're not truly comfortable with everything you see in the mirror, then you're not really on stage at all. Your shadow is.

THE PARADOX OF PERSONAL VALUE

THIS ONE IS ARGUABLY the most important thing I have learned in my life, when it comes to navigating a life within a career. That means this chapter is about the one thing above of all that made me understand how to succeed in the industry I was in, but also how to avoid growing bitter from all the rejection that comes with a life in my business. It's my one true gold-nugget on how to have a successful career and have a happy life at the same time. Obviously, being so terribly important, this chapter will probably not be the last you hear of this, but let's see how the book unfolds. I call it the paradox of personal value.

Personal value really has become the new black within the corporate world in recent years. It's also referred to as emotional intelligence. Personally, I don't think the two are the same. I'm not even convinced emotional intelligence exists. It may just be a fancy marriage of two words to describe something that is basically empathy or sympathy in the workplace. However, personal value does exist in a work situation. Sounds awfully important, right? Well, it is. It's what a lot of companies are buzzing about in order to establish stronger bonds with customers to ensure a more stable income, because you want, as a business, to be able to rely on your customers to continuously throw their business your way. Many leaders have already figured out that this comes from gaining more personal relationships with customers; making the customers feel like they're a friend of the company; part of the family. Being able to use personality in business is... well... the shit. If a customer wishes to buy a good bottle of wine, you could just order it online and have it shipped, but if you have the option of going to the local wine dealer, where the owner is this wonderful, charismatic person, and it always ends up in an interesting little conversation about wine and life; you always leave in a slightly better mood, just because you like the person, the dealer, know the names of the dealer's three illegitimate but charming children, and you leave with the same wine you could have bought online, and maybe even more wine than you had planned. The point is, the wine is not really the product. The person behind the counter selling the love of wine is the product.

On stage, and especially in theatre, where I come from, this mechanism is amplified by ten. At least. In most businesses, like the wine dealer, you have a tangible product, and if someone asks what the company sells, you can show them a picture of your product being wine, cars, food, insurances, computers, tiny parts for computers, tiny parts for cars, tax returns, coffins, biscuits, et cetera. And whoever shows the picture is often overlooked and forgotten. If someone asked me what my product was, I would have to show them my passport and the very unattractive picture of me inside it. When you're on stage, when you're an entrepreneur, when you're a speaker, *you* are the product. Just like the actors of the play, each and individually, is the product. And then at the same time we're not, and THIS is where the paradox comes in. The paradox of personal value.

When I go on stage as an actor, then I am not myself on stage, unlike the employee who stands up at the company meeting to deliver their presentation. I, as an actor, am whatever role is required of me to pretend to be within the script of that particular play. And the play is the product. Not me. Unless it was a one man show, a concert or a stand-up gig the play is the product. The production is the product. I just play my part as the piece of the puzzle within the product of the show. However, if I do not invest myself personally in the role I play; if I do not allow myself to get emotionally attached to the role, and let it almost consume me, it will not feel authentic and plausible to the audience/consumers, they will not connect with my role, and it will simply not be interesting to them. If you, as an actor, fail to be interesting on stage, you have failed all together. It is necessary for me to contribute my personal value to the product of the show, to make it interesting to the audience/customers. I have to be happy and sad up there. I have to be brave, vulnerable, frightened and elated. I may even have to draw on personal memories of childhood traumas, loss of loved ones, my first kiss, my first love to win the audience over.

The world in which we all go to work every day, wherever and whatever our work may be, is one big corporate theatre, and accepting that it's theatre doesn't mean we have surrendered to the dark side or partnered with the devil. At the end of the day, I'm still just playing my part to make the product interesting enough for the customers to buy it. AND here is where it really sucks sometimes, while getting really interesting at the same time. I have to add personal value to the product, in order to persuade the customers to buy it.

BUT if they did not like the product, being the play in my case, it's not for me to take personally. It was not really me up there, so it's not me as a person they didn't like, and that is fine. They just did not like the product. Personal value is your way to make your customers interested in your product. Any customer is more likely to buy, when they get emotionally connected with the product. Now, that will not happen with a bottle of wine that you buy online, because the bottle itself can't show emotion, but the dealer at the shop can. So, as soon as you can accept that adding yourself to the mix in an honest, truthful way, you increase the potential of success of whatever business you're in. When I say *adding yourself honestly*, it's because you may have been on those holidays typically around the Mediterranean Sea, where the restaurants line the boardwalk of the harbour. Obnoxious waiters are practically attacking you in the middle of the street, to haul you into their respective food establishment, to a point where you may eat there once, because you're too shy of conflict to refuse, but never set foot on that entire street again out of fear of culinary assault. That's what I mean. You have to add yourself into the mix in an HONEST and TRUTHFUL way. Because, honestly, that was not the best restaurant in town.

To sum up the paradox. You increase your chance of success in business exponentially by daring to be personal and invest yourself emotionally in both your product and how you communicate with your customers. However, if they dislike your product, do not take it personally. It was not you as a person they didn't like. It was your product and your communication of it. All you can do is to go back to the drawing board, look at the product and how you sold it. Maybe you had the best of intentions of being personal, but ended up pulling *a Mediterranean waiter*, and scared them away instead. Maybe you were a Brazilian working in Denmark. In your home culture you were perceived as one of the soft ones, but in another culture, you are suddenly the pushy, obnoxious showoff. You could say that you have to be personal objectively. Invest as much of yourself emotionally and personally in what you do, but do it, bearing in mind, what serves the product and what serves the customer. If they still won't buy, look at the product. Not at yourself. Unless you take it personally. If so, see the next chapter. If you start by being personal in your own life, what that means is you decide to be open about viewing your own personality. You can't really be personal, without being honest with yourself about what your personality comprises. Good or bad. As a benefit of this you develop a self-awareness of gaining perspective about who you are as a person and how you project your personality, but more importantly, how your personality is viewed by others. And it's ultimately how others perceive you that determines your success both in your life and in your business. You can think you're one hell of a fantastic human being, with an amazing sense of humour and compassionate personality, but if others see you differently; sees you as an asshole, then to them you are an asshole. Sorry. However, the cool benefit of gaining a higher self-awareness about your own personality is that you also learn to read the personality of others better. Meaning, you can gain a higher skill for understanding your customers and what will make them buy your product, because here is the cool thing about the psychology of personality: By understanding someone's personality, you can learn to predict their behaviour.

If you get personal in business, two things will happen. 1) Your customers will engage in your company, because they will care about your product, and 2) Your boss, your colleagues, your sub-contractors, what have you, will actually want to work with you. Not just because they appreciate your personal commitment to the business and your shared endeavours into creating a great product, but also because they want to know how your three illegitimate but charming children are doing.

13

YOUR NEED FOR TAKING SHIT
PERSONALLY

THE PRODUCT HAS no value if you're not personal, BUT if the audience does not like the product, it's not to be taken personally. If I did anyway, as an artist, I had two choices: Try to see the audience's point of view for not liking the product or look myself in the mirror and ask:

"What is this need you have for taking it personally?"

The fact remained. I was just not a good or interesting enough product.

The paradox of personal value really is a fickle beast. It can be very powerful when you put it to the right use. It can also cause terrible havoc to your life if you don't learn to control the beast and manage it to your advantage.

If you, despite my recommendations, do take criticism personally; if you do get offended by someone else having seemingly negative things to say about your accomplishments, what is that all about? Why do you take it personally? Well, it's not because there is something inherently wrong with you as a person. Unfortunately, it is also not because the person giving you negative criticism is an idiot. Sometimes they are, but it doesn't help you in performing better to insist on that. It also doesn't make you any more at peace with yourself, to claim that the person was indeed an idiot. The only thing that will help you is to accept that if you get offended by criticism and take things personally, it is because you have a need for taking shit personally. Which means, you have to figure out what the need is all about and where it comes from. If you struggle with taking criticism personally, you definitely should have a chat with your therapist, but there's a good chance it has something to do with you having a conviction of low self-esteem. When I say, *conviction of*, it's because I don't believe *self-esteem* exists. I certainly have seen no proper proof of its existence, or any reason we should take this construct seriously. Which could mean, maybe what's holding you back is just an illusion? Do you have low self-esteem, or are you merely a slave to a bad idea?

14

THE WORTHLESS PURSUIT OF SELF-ESTEEM

LET us glimpse at this strange concept. Not for long, just enough to rattle your world a little. We've got other matters to attend to, besides meddling with your belief system.

Self-esteem, what is that other than two words put together? What does it mean? It means, what you think of yourself. Your overall evaluation and appraisal of your own worth. How you value yourself. If you were to sell yourself, what price would you put on yourself? Are you worthless or priceless? It doesn't mean whether you're happy. It doesn't mean that you're confident. It doesn't mean that you behave well or treat others nicely. It simply means that you have a low regard or a high regard for your own worth. We all want high self-esteem, but that means you think highly of yourself. It doesn't sound so attractive, when I put it that way, does it? It suddenly sounds like you are a little full of yourself. That's why it is so strange to me, why this concept has become so important for so many people, and why so many, especially girls and young women, spend so much time trying to obtain it, because at the same time, we make a virtue out of modesty and humility. And it's so strange why people torment themselves for having too low self-esteem. Who says that low self-esteem is a bad thing? Having high self-esteem does not make you a pleasant person. How you behave makes you a pleasant person. In fact, the latest studies on this concept, yet to be proved existing, show that young people who spend a lot of time trying to boost their self-esteem end up narcissistic. Also, bullies have not only high but also surprisingly and inappropriately high self-esteem (regard for themselves). That is why they can bully, because they feel entitled to do it. They think that much of themselves. Of course, it doesn't mean that they are happy individuals deep down. Of course not. That's why pursuing self-esteem is worthless.

I can't see how ascribing a worth to yourself has any purpose. It would for 12-year-old Sporus, when Emperor Nero bought him around the year AD 65 to be his favourite sex-slave, substitute wife and treated him like a being without either soul, mind or emotion. Then it would be fair to say that the poor boy was worth more than that. Apart from human trafficking, inherent human worth has no context. And we, as people, don't have an inherent worth just because we're human. There's no species on the planet that has behaved more appallingly and atrociously throughout the better part of our existence than the humans. We treat each other appallingly, the planet appallingly and all other species on it appallingly. So, no, we don't have an inherent value for being human. Furthermore, if you think about it, every time you hear someone trying to describe their self-esteem, they will say something like, *my self-esteem is generally okay,* or *sometimes good or pretty bad...* but they will also say that sometimes it changes or varies. If they are asked one day where everything is awesome; their video on Insta got 1000 hearts, they got the job or passed the exam, then they will describe their self-esteem as high. They never describe an actual value or worth of themselves, because they can't. It is too elusive. They just describe how they feel. When they talk about self-esteem, what they are describing is usually just their mood. And we can't attribute the existence of something regarded so valuable and important as self-esteem on something as capricious as our own individual subjective feelings. Feelings are much too fickle for that. Feelings change. Constantly. And if you say, *but I have had low self-esteem and felt worthless most of my life*, it still does not mean that self-esteem exists. You have just created a narrative, a story of yourself that you have told yourself for years. A story you are unwilling to change. It's more than 20 years ago that Tony Robbins coined the phrase: *The story you tell yourself is the life you lead*. Start telling yourself a different story!

Why would you want to prioritise how much you think of yourself over how you behave, what you think you can do and what you think of others?

If I told you that having low self-esteem has nothing to do with whether you are happy in your life, would that be of importance to you? Would it rattle your world a little? If so, good. Then think about it for a while. If you have confidence problems, and you're afraid to get up and perform, it has nothing to with what you think of yourself. You may blame your lack of performance on your poor view of yourself, but that's entirely your choice. If you improve your view of your own worth, it doesn't necessarily make you perform any more admirably or any better, and it certainly does not guarantee happiness or success. What you need to get up there and speak is confidence, competence and preparation.

Even if you're only too aware that you think badly of yourself, is that so awful? I say, it's better than thinking too much of yourself, because thinking little of yourself will make you reflect. It will make you look in the mirror. It will make you see other people for who they are. And when you see how they respond to you coming at them with your modest sense of self-worth, you will find:

You are not what you value yourself to be. You are what you have been shaped to be as a child and how you behave as an adult.
Self-esteem does not exist.

15

MEMORISED SPEECH VS. STRUCTURED SPEECH

Acting vs. Speaking

WHEN I COACH PUBLIC-SPEAKING, especially if it's one on one, the one thing that seems to dominate my trainees the most, apart from the fear of speaking itself, is the fear of acting. For some reason, many people think acting is the equivalent of failing as a speaker. This could not be further from the truth.

They link it directly to a false conviction that acting equals coming off as fake or pretend. Incredible. So, when I go into full director mode with them, and get really nerdy with the details, I always, without exception, have to explain myself at some point in the process, for them to accept the validity of the tools I am giving them. Let's say, they come to me with a speech they are preparing to give at work, and they want my help. We have immersed ourselves into the process. We have established the structure of the speech. The ethos, pathos, and logos are all mapped out. The material is good. The story is strong. The information is delivered. We are at the point where the speaker is going back and forth over one little paragraph, trying to get to the absolute authentic core of what is said. I ask the speaker to stop at a certain word, think about the word or the memory that lies behind the word, look at the audience with intent, wait for the response, and then move on. It reaches a level of consciousness, where the speaker inevitably stops and says: *I'm struggling with this, because I feel like I'm just acting.* Meaning, to the speaker, this is a bad thing. Then, of course, I scoff overly dramatically and with an Ian McKellen type voice sarcastically exclaim: *"JUST acting? JUST... ACTING???"* If you are diving into what feels like acting, it means you are diving into the most complex layer of public speaking. The layer which will take you from a good speaker, maybe even a great speaker, to a one-in-a-thousand outstanding speaker.

You are diving into the understanding of how human beings behave unconsciously, while being able to replicate that on a conscious level; the incredibly fascinating work of acting! Because here is the deal: When you start to feel like you're acting, you automatically assume that your audience will think it looks like acting too. You become self-aware of the mechanics that lie behind your delivery, which, temporarily, makes it feel fake to you. Thus, you assume that your audience will also feel the mechanics, and think you're a fake, and yes, that can happen... if you're a BAD actor. But it's only temporarily. Hopefully. You're practicing, so everything will and should feel strange and unfamiliar. Whatever feels strange, your entire system will automatically combat and assume to be wrong, simply because it feels unfamiliar. We are unbelievable creatures of habit. Do not forget that. You're just practicing. If what you do, while practicing, doesn't feel wrong, then you're doing something wrong. As Michael Jackson always said during his rehearsals to the poor backup dancers and musicians, desperately trying to keep up with his genius: *That's what rehearsals are for. This is where you do it wrong. With the love. (to be said with a kinaes-*

thetic, high-pitched, child-like voice) You don't go in front of the board room or in front of the crowd, up on stage, unprepared. That would be unbelievably foolish. You practise. You study the intricacies of how people behave and respond, and in the practice, it will feel unnatural, fake and wrong. It will feel like bad acting. So, you keep practicing. Hopefully you didn't procrastinate and put off preparing the speech until the day before. When you finally do take to the stage, it no longer feels like bad acting. It feels natural, conscious, powerful, truthful and amazing. You feel every bit is real as you, the student of speech, standing here in front of me living and breathing, while I explain acting to you.

You remember the guy I told you about earlier, who emotionally broke down on stage in the middle of his speech about the struggles of philosophy? He had done his homework. He had studied. He had practiced. He had rehearsed. He had gone through all the phases of frustration, trying to get to the core of what he really wanted to communicate, and what was really in his heart. He was confident that public speaking could not kill him. The very day before the day of his speech, he gave a last rehearsal of it. It was good, but settled. He had decided that this was how he would do it, and he was fine with that. I knew, though, if he went on stage like that, he would do a great but composed and ultimately less inspiring speech. So, I pushed him. I questioned his authenticity. I questioned his very enthusiasm and motivation for being up there. I told him it sounded in his voice like he was just not all that enthusiastic about being up there. He argued that he couldn't be enthusiastic about being up there all the time. Some memories he shared were terrible memories to him, so he couldn't be enthusiastic in the middle of a terrible memory. I countered that regardless of the memory you share, you still have to be enthusiastic about wanting to share it with the audience. You are not up there for your own therapeutic purposes. If you can't be enthusiastic on behalf of the audience at every step of the way, then you don't belong up there. Do it for them and be there for them. I could see the frustration in his eyes from being questioned so close to the event. I knew he could handle it, though. I knew his safety net was in place. The preparation had been done. I knew he was ready to take all that preparation and just... let go. And the next night he did. All the preparation was there. The speech was tight, well crafted, well executed, but right in the centre of it was his true authentic self. Brave and vulnerable, letting it all go, without fully knowing but trusting that the preparation, the mechanics, the work would carry him home to safe shores. It did. No one saw the mechanics. They just saw him.

A good actor can make you not see the mechanics, and persuade you that the role they're playing, is a real person living and breathing right here, right now, in this world with you in the audience. They can make you forget time and place and suck you into a world of emotion and voluntary imagination. They do that with honesty and authenticity to themselves, while they're in the role. If they're too hung up on, let's say, impressing the audience, it will amount to nothing but a bunch of skills and mechanics, and it will show. The actor who is up there, with an honest wish to be there for the audience, will commit themselves willingly to the role. They will invest themselves emotionally in the role, for the sake of making it authentic and credible to the audience. The same goes for speakers.

Acting and public speaking is the same!

But when I'm speaking, I'm not playing a role! I don't want to play a role. I don't want to act. It's me at work giving a presentation. It's me at TEDx doing my first talk about real life. No, it is not! Sorry to burst your bubble. The only time when it is real life, as it comes to speaking, is when you are speaking without any prior thought or preparation to what you were going to say. The spontaneous conversation. This is not it. Whatever scenario you can conjure up in your mind, that you could call public speaking, is not real life. You have prepared. You have structured. You have given thought to what you're going to say, why you're saying it, and what you want the outcome of your speaking to be. Whether it's a huge speaking event on stage with lots of production, a wedding speech or a business presentation at work, what you're doing is delivery. A performance, so I'm sorry, my dear, you are now in the wonderful realm of acting. Accept it. This could be the beginning of a beautiful friendship. It's really cool here and so much more fun, once you accept that. Here's looking at you, kid.

So, with that in mind, let's look at the difference between, what I call, a structured speech and a memorised speech.

- **The structured speech requires nothing but you. Speaking skills are advised. (achievable in a month)**
- **The memorised speech requires acting skills. Speaking skills are advised. (years of training to be expected)**

Basically, a memorised speech is what the actor does every time, without exception. You have a script, and you learn it by heart. Word for Word. Then you prepare it meticulously and deliver it to the audience verbatim, as in the script. The structured speech is when you don't write the entire speech out and memorise it, but you create a structure for the speech, and you memorise the structure. A structured speech is what a speaker always should opt for, if in any way possible. The structured speech still leaves room for a natural sense of spontaneity. You can still feel real in a structured speech; feel like it's you just talking and coming up with half of it on the go. You can incorporate a certain amount of speaking skills (only a certain amount. We'll get back to that), but still maintain your own raw sense of authenticity.

If you, as part of your speech, are sharing a personal story from your past, to communicate a point, even if you've never told the story before, you don't have to write it down, because you were there. You will always remember your own story. Regardless how many times you tell it, it will always sound like the first time, because you never wrote it down and scripted it. As soon as you script your speech, you move into an area, where you have to know, at every level, how a human being behaves, delivers words and sentences, how eye contact correlates with what we say, et cetera, in order to not look like a robot on stage, and that is what actors do and spend years on mastering. If you write an entire speech down and memorise it, then know that this is the game you signed up for.

Also, there is nothing like a memorised speech that can spark an anxiety attack from expected failure rivalled only by apocalypse and the foreseeable doom of your entire being. There is nothing that can terrify like the fear of simply forgetting your words, because if the foundation of your speech rests on your words and you forget them, you're screwed. Another grand reason to avoid this option, if possible.

The Memorised Speech

For obvious reasons, I will not go into detail about how

to achieve greatness in the memorised speech. I will always try to persuade you away from it, anyway. Should you have the odd need for a memorised speech – say you are entering a speech contest with a 5-7-minute timeframe, and you get disqualified if you exceed the limit by 30 seconds, your awareness of time management thus forcing you to script and memorise your speech, so you can time it within ten seconds, well, then call me. In that case, we have a lot to do in the acting department, and this was not supposed to be a book about acting, but communication and our ability for such.

16

HOW TO CRAFT A WELL-STRUCTURED SPEECH

BEFORE WE CRAFT THE SPEECH, you must first make some decisions. What are the strategic objectives of your speech? YOUR purpose. This means crafting the speech is about what you want the audience to take away from the speech. The value of the speech to the audience. The entire process of crafting the speech itself is about making sure the audience takes away something of value. But there's a reason you're getting up there in the first place. Why? What are your personal reasons for getting up there? What's your endgame? And I say reasons, because there should be more than one. These are your strategic objectives. There are both short-term strategic objectives and long-term strategic objectives.

If you're doing a presentation at work, your short-term objective is likely obvious. Your boss told you to do this presentation. So, the short-term objective is to do the presentation well enough to not get fired. However, long term, you may want to advance in the business. You may want to use your presentation as part of a plan to develop a whole new business model. Maybe you want to inspire your boss and the surrounding team to embrace and further a different mindset about how they relate to what you can contribute with, and that might be included in how you package your whole presentation. If you're doing the wedding speech, decide if you want to make them laugh or cry, because doing both and everything in between could prove a mistake, if you're not the most experienced of speakers. If you're doing that first and oh, so elusive TEDx Talk, what do you want to happen afterwards? Do you want to do more TED Talks? Do you want to sell the idea you shared? Do you just want to inspire, and if so, for what reason? Do you want to launch a podcast a month later and draw attention towards that? Yes, I know, sometimes you are asked by your boss to do a presentation, you have an hour to prepare, and the reason or desired outcome of the presentation can seem as clear as muddy water in back-alley puddle but, nonetheless. Decide, before turning your full focus to the audience, what you want to achieve by getting up there.

MAIN STRUCTURE

This is our primary domain of focus for this book. How to communicate with competence and consideration to a strategic objective. You have a purpose with your intended communication, so how do you prepare that with the least amount of horrific fear of speaking to follow? You build as strong a structure as possible with least amount of memorisation. Basically, the structured speech should go like this:

- **Strong opening/Ethos. Who am I? Why am I here, and why should you listen?**
- **Middle/Pathos. The emotionally engaging narrative.**
- **Awe-inspiring end/Logos. The core message. Take-away. Call to action**

OPENING

A strong opening is absolutely crucial. There are several things you have to achieve in the opening of your speech, but it boils down to the fundamental first criterion of public speaking, mentioned in the beginning. Be able to keep their attention. Your opening has to be so good and interesting that it will make the listener want to stay through the whole thing. Make them want to stay with YOU, and listen to YOU... until you stop talking, which is a near impossible thing to do. So, no pressure, but your opening is mightily important. Before we move on with your jaw-dropping opening, maybe I should specify what I mean by opening, meaning how long is an opening. If it was on social media, where all words that create attraction and views are accompanied by still-images or video, you have 3-5 seconds to hook the viewer. This is a medium getting almost impossible to navigate, for appalling reasons. We'll get back to that too. Here, we focus on live communication, meaning face-to-face communication; you, talking in front of other people, actually there in the room with you. In a public live speech, your opening is:

3 sentences, tops!

That's it. *Well, what constitutes a sentence duration wise?* Yeah, yeah, smarty pants. Of course, if your opening has really short punchy sentences, you can bump it up to 4-5 sentences. Let's say four lines of text in a word document font size 12. Happy? Good.

Apart from getting your listeners plain interested, what else do you need to achieve in measly four lines of text? A lot.

What are you talking about?

First, make them know right off the bat, why they're there. What is this going to be about... Exactly? And don't fool them. Don't play clever little games with them, thinking, *I'll start with this setup, and then later I'll surprise them, make a twist and a turn, and magically unfold the actual message to them. They'll be mesmerised.* No, they will not. They will be confused, and you will lose their attention. If you want to play games with people, write a novel and go nuts with the plot twists. Tell them exactly what the subject of the speech will be about. A fantastic tip to achieve this is to have one word that embodies your message and use that word one or more times in the opening sentences. We call this *priming*. You can prime people's minds by subconsciously preparing their minds to think in a certain way, by using words that corresponds directly and emotionally with the mindset of your topic.

Why you?

Second, make them understand who you are up there as a speaker. Your **ethos**. Your credibility. Why is it you up there, speaking about this topic, and not someone else; someone more competent or experienced with the subject-matter than you. Stand out immediately as an authority in your speech. At a corporate meeting, the accountant should be the authority on explaining the quarterly result of the business, but you have to let them know that that is who you are, so they damn well better listen. If you're giving a speech to the groom at the wedding, it's not the fact that they invited you to the wedding, which makes you an authority on sharing personal stories about the groom's embarrassing past. It's the fact that you have known him all your life. If you tell them, they will assume there are interesting stories in the pipeline, and they will listen.

The Hook

Third, hook them onto the story of this speech itself, so they will get excited about the potential of staying around until the end to see where this is going, and how it all ends. The movie trailer version of this is the cliffhanger where you leave the audience hanging with some question they will be dying to have answered, or some piece of information, so puzzling and intriguing, they have to hear more.

"… they have uncovered the potential bloodline of Jesus Christ."

They have what???… How did they do that, and what does that even mean? This is of course the plot of The Da Vinci Code by Dan Brown, which currently resides as #11 on the list of best-selling books of all time world-wide. Yes, THE best-selling list. The one that has the Bible as #1 with 5 billion copies sold, Don Quixote #2 with 500 million sold, followed by Dickens, Tolkien, Saint-Exupéry, Christie, Lewis et cetera, and the reason for the astounding success of the book is that the very idea of the plot is so intriguing on so many levels. Whether you have any interest in Christianity, you just have to know what he's talking about, when he says: *A bloodline of Jesus Christ.* That's a cliffhanger at its most sophisticated. It's not just the literal cliff-hanger, where we will cut away from someone hanging off a cliff, making you want to know if he dies or not, but something that makes you wonder. Something that sets your imagination on fire. THAT is a good opening.

To recap, make them interested, let them know what's

coming, establish your ethos, and get them hooked. Ethos can be established in many ways, and of course it depends on what kind of speech you're giving, to whom, with what purpose, and what you want the outcome to be. What is the perfect opening, you ask? There is no such thing, as perfection does not exist. Everything is subjective to your situation, and everything is a matter of taste, anyway. We can never make everyone like us all the time. All we can do is to optimise our craft as much as possible to cover as many factors as we can, and thus appeal to as many people as possible.

Nonetheless, I will give you an example. I was giving a speech a while back about *freedom of speech*, within the debate of political correctness, and the impact of the latter on free speech. I chose to set up the speech as if it was a eulogy at a funeral. The speech started like this:

Example of a good opening

"I really did not want to say anything here today, as this is a moment where no one wants to speak. We have lost a friend. To me a loved one. We're only a small gathering today, but so many people befriended this person over the years. His name was Free Speech. ..."

- *Martin Svaneborg*

This is a pretty good opening to a speech, if I am to say so myself, with an Iron Man sort of complete lack of modesty. Let me briefly point of what we achieved in these modest four lines:

- It makes you **interested** or puzzled in the very first

sentenced, by saying that *no one wants to speak in this moment*. You immediately think: *What moment and why not?*

- I answer your immediate **why** *you are here* by saying: *We have lost a friend.* WE. Including you. That's why you're here.

- I establish my **ethos** of credibility/why am I giving the eulogy instead of you? *To me, a loved one.* Meaning, to you a friend, but I knew him intimately.

- I tell you, discretely, **what** this speech will be about: The impact of free speech on all of our lives (*so many people befriended this person*). Both you here today, and everyone else have known and had their lives impacted so profoundly by free speech that you ended up regarding him a friend.

- **The hook**. This is the magical touch. Instead of talking about *free speech* as an intellectual concept of communication, I personify *free speech* and even claim his death. *His name was Free Speech.* The philosophy geeks will notice the reference to Nietzsche claiming, "God is dead", and get a kick out of that. Everyone else will respond instinctively to this drawing threads back deep into our human history of mythological archetypes, good and evil fighting for the balance between order and chaos. These narratives of archetypes are what our civilised world is built on, from ancient narratives like Moses being cast into chaos, having to lead his people back to enlightenment and order, to modern tales, where Disney's The Lion King is a prime example. The wise and kind king, Mufasa, is the ruler of order. *All that light falls upon is yours*, meaning all that you can grasp and understand is your enlightened order. Your consciousness. You have freedom within the enlightenment. But what happens if Mufasa dies? Chaos and darkness will inevitably ensue. The concept of free speech is deeply rooted in our understanding of our species and our definition of the world and society we live in. Just the word *freedom* itself has such a grip on us that the very mention of its absence will thrust a surge of fear into the pit of your stomach. What constitutes a good, happy, prospering world is our freedom to communicate, share ideas, and to stay true to our own hearts. If free speech is dead, it means we are hurled collectively and instantaneously into an abyss of chaos, and something near divine would be necessary to pull us out of that dark pit of despair. With this one sentence, I force you to ask yourself two questions, you really don't want to ask, but faced by them must have answered. 1) If free speech is dead, what does that mean, and how will it affect my life, and in these times of trending sexism, the more important 2) HIS name...? Who the f... says free speech was a man?

Not bad to achieve all of that in less than four lines, wouldn't you say? Fundamentally, these four lines should make you want to stay, and hopefully, right now, as you read this, you are thinking: *Damn. I wish he had included the rest of the speech. I want to see how it ended.* Mission Opening accomplished.

Another example of a great opening is from my favourite speech of all time, and yes, it comes from acting and not from real life. At is the ending of the movie, The Dictator, by Charlie Chaplin:

"I'm sorry, but I don't want to be an emperor. That's not my business. I don't want to rule or conquer anyone. I should like to help everyone - if possible - Jew, Gentile, black man, white. We all want to help one another. Human beings are like that."

– *Charlie Chaplin*

Apart from this being so beautifully written it brings tears to my eyes, it is the supreme example of ethos. He talks about abolishing dictatorship in the world, AND HE IS ONE. Who could be more credible to talk about how to create liberty and justice for all than an ex-dictator? So, for an emperor to get up and say, *I'm sorry, I don't want to be an emperor. That's not my business...* that's one hell of an opening.

The Middle
The pathos/ the personal story

This is where we get personal, but before we do that, we have to go way back in our human history. To the very dawn of our species. We don't have to stay there long. It's just to give you a timeline but also a sense of the time-span in which our capacity for speech and communication has evolved. Our fondness of public speaking is not something that grew into our world since the advent of Tony Robbins.

Geoffrey Finch has written a brilliant book called *Word of Mouth*, about the evolution of language. Worth reading. He opens the book by posing the interesting question: What would you suggest being the most significant invention ever by humankind? Most people would say, wielding fire, the invention of the wheel, the book press, or some scientific or technological advancement like modern vaccine, birth control, microprocessors, et cetera. Few people would argue for the invention of language, and this is probably because it is not part of our human history to regard language as an invention. For millennia, language was seen as something that was given to us by a divine power, and not something we made on our own. But as Finch so rightfully points out, no other invention would have been possible without the initial invention of language. Archeology is proving more and more strongly that language developed out of a necessity for communication on an ever more sophisticated level. With the expansion of our human brain over millions of years, and our subsequent development as a more advanced being, so too developed a need for more advanced capabilities for communication. The actual arrival of language is said to lie somewhere between the year 250.000-100.000 BC.

Why is this important to the pathos of our story? Because to argue why pathos, being the emotional connection, is the right choice for the middle part of our speech, we have to understand what we, as people, are best programmed to connect with the most, when it comes to communication. What we're most likely, collectively, to respond positively to. What is our history of how we, as humans, have passed on information from person to person, and from generation to generation? I will not bore you with too much data, so let's keep it really simple.

About a hundred-thousand years ago we sat around a campfire, after the hunt of the day had ended. Stories were shared about how the day went. This served multiple purposes. The obvious purpose of passing on life or death information to the other hunters and the families back in the camp about what pitfalls and dangers they had encountered, and how to avoid such dangers in the future. It also served as a social glue, bonding the people of the tribe together, to share the personal stories and reactions of the day passed.

Roughly five-thousand years ago, writing was invented, and from then on it took over, as our way of passing on information from generation to generation. Not because of the social significance of writing, but because the information could be preserved on paper (in multiple stages of invention) beyond the span of a lifetime. The person with the knowledge, the information, and the wisdom, did not have to be alive for the communication to be passed on.

In 1987, Microsoft software developers, Robert Gaskins and Dennis Austin invented PowerPoint. So, I ask you. PowerPoint – with a few decades of human use, the written word – with about 5.000 years of human use, or the campfire story – with 100.000-250.000 years of human use: Which one do you think we are most deeply and powerfully programmed to respond to? Bingo! The campfire story. That is the reason why pathos is the middle part of our speech. The story and the middle of our speech has to be personal if in any way possible (and it is in 99,8% of the time), because it will make the audience connect on a very deep level, reaching hundreds of thousands of years into our ancestral past. If you master the personal campfire story, they will ultimately care.

Let's get the burning objection out of the way, before we get to a really good personal story. Right now, you're internally jumping up and down, with a figurative finger jabbing furiously into imaginary air saying, "But I can't always get a personal story into a speech! Especially if it's a business presentation. Sometimes there are just facts and information needed to be conveyed, and there is nothing personal about it...?"

Right and wrong.

Sometimes there is no way to add a personal story from

your own life, to connect with the overall message of your speech, but there is always a way to be personal with how you convey the otherwise dry facts and figures you have to present. Before, I used the example of the accountant having to present the quarterly result. That was intentional, because the very competent Canadian speaker, Eric Edmeades, did a great course in public speaking once (you may still find it on the almighty interweb), where he used this very example. So, this is me, paraphrasing Eric Edmeades, just because I can't come up with a better example.

An accountant presents the results of the past quarter in front of the board and most of the company.

Scenario A:

"Ladies and gentlemen, I am here to present the result. We projected a 14% growth on the quarter, and I am happy to tell you, we achieved 16% growth on the quarter."

Not bad, right? In fact, many presentations will be much worse, with a bunch of *ehs* and *uhms* mixed into the palette.

Scenario B:

"Ladies and gentlemen, I don't know if you remember, when, a year ago, a 14% growth was projected for this quarter. I actually did not believe that was possible, given the state of our industry and the world at present. So, yesterday, when they handed me this envelope I hold in my hand, and I read the numbers, I hesitated to believe it, so I read it again. I read it a third time. Because of X, Y and Z we have not only achieved 14% growth. Ladies and gentlemen, we have achieved 16% growth on the quarter."

YES, all you reality-seeking business people out there, you can argue that this is not a credible example. The accountant would not be surprised. He would have known how the numbers were turning out, and the accountant should be fired if there was no belief in the goals of the company. That's not the point. If someone asks you the next day, what was said at the presentation, which one would you remember the best? Scenario B! Of course, because, though there was no personal story, it was made personal anyway. The narrative became personal. Even though you, the accountant, knew exactly what was in the envelope and had known for weeks, you could act surprised. Just for the engagement of it; for the sake of making your colleagues care. That's what Scenario B did. There was even suspense created, which made you much more excited about the result.

With that point made, I hope we can agree that any speech can have a personal story integrated, and the more personal and the more unique to you, the more the audience will bond with you. The story I told you in the beginning about my debut on the stage and the crappy director, is one I could use to talk about a multitude of different topics. I can make several points with that story. I could make a point about how to overcome obstacles and adversity in life. I could make one about the importance of empathy. I could make one about how to gain perspective. I could even make one about the purposes for the choices we make in life. So, it's a great story to have in the journal. It's also a quite deep and emotional story. The whole first act of this book was in fact a speech in itself, with a nice opening, a really good story, and a message at the end of act 1, about how it's never too late to learn and just because something you have experienced is ten years in the past doesn't mean you can't keep learning from that experience for the rest of your life. Uh, me likes a nice long sentence.

Sabina and the catastrophic kiss

When I was in tenth grade, I was in a youth drama group. There, I encountered Sabina. The enchanting, enthralling, intoxicating, enslaving goddess of beauty, sexuality, maturity and awesomeness, Sabina. I fell head over heels in love. Have you guessed? Clever you. She was tall. She had long dark wavy hair, long, slender legs, a body I can't even begin to describe, and a personality that could charm anyone. Especially teenage boys.

We were in this drama group together. The following year, I was a first year in college, and we had, for some strange reason unbeknownst to me, stayed in touch. Sabina had become assistant director of the drama group, which I was no longer a part of, and invited me to come see their new play. Of course, I did. I don't remember the play at all, even though it was opening night. Probably because I had no interest in the play whatsoever.

After the performance, I was invited to join them for the after party, and this is where the potential magic began. At some point the after party turned into the entire group, Sabina and I sitting on the floor in a big circle playing *Spin the bottle*; either an ingenious or deeply traumatising game, where, when it's your turn to spin the bottle, everyone else decides what you should do either to or with the person, whom the bottle points at. It goes without saying that when the game is played by twenty teenagers infused by a growing level of alcohol, the decisions always turn into an escalating daring game of naughty and semi-erotic exploration. Let's just say that the third time it was my turn, the game had reached body-tequila level. I don't remember the second turn. However, the first time it was my turn, the entire cosmos suddenly swirled with awe-inspiring power, pulling entire suns and moons around, and aligned into a potential gateway to Nirvana. The group decided that whoever the bottle pointed at; I should kiss. At about 330° North-west sat Sabina. This was it. I had no interest in the foolishness of the teenage games of exploration. The adolescent naiveté of my boyish crush only had one thing in mind: The elusive, heavenly salvation of Sabina's kiss. The perfect kiss that would inevitably make her fall madly in love with me too. If the stars were aligned and the universe on my side, the bottle would point to her. Not *at* her. *TO* her. Of course. What do you take me for? Some second rate high-school poet? Internal scoff. There were roughly twenty people in the 360° circle; of course, it would stop within the 10° that held the portal to my heavenly kingdom. On the eastern side of the circle, were about five or six other boys. I would rather not kiss them. No offense. I stood up, dusted myself off, and got ready to leave this world behind. I stepped into the circle with as much fake confidence as I could muster, crouched down, grabbed the bottled, and gave it a swirl. I fixed my eyes on the bottle, as it turned furiously for what felt like an eternity. As it slowed, images of Nirvana flashed before my eyes with increasing clarity. Of course, images of the potential first encounters with the pleasures of homosexuality also flashed by with equal clarity. It seemed like the bottle would never stop, and during the last excruciating turn it was as if the bottle was deliberately taunting me, having made up its wine-smelling mind about my fate. The bottled stopped. It STOPPED. The world stopped as the bottle pointed, not indecisively in between two people, but directly at the goddess.

I looked up. I looked at her, and the daunting effect of her gaze pierced me as her eyes met mine. There was a look of exhilarated expectation in those eyes. I tried to hide my euphoria. My rite of passage into manhood lay before me. The universe had spoken, and the decision was indisputable. I had to leave the centre of the circle for a moment before facing my fate, so I turned my back on Sabina, and walked back to my spot at the edge of the circle. I had to brace myself. It was like another scene from that fantastic movie, *Love, Actually*, when Laura Linney's character finally brings home the enigmatic hunk of a chief designer, Carl, after the Christmas party. In the doorway, she stops him and says, "Can you just wait for one moment?" She goes around the corner and two steps up the stairs, where she silently screams in excitement over the prospect of the caramel-coloured GOD waiting by her door. I was Laura Linney in that moment.

The moment had arrived. I turned with conviction and walked over to Sabina. During the 40-year-desert-like hike there, Sabina cried out:

"Come on, Martin. You're gonna get kissed."

I nearly stumbled, but I got out of the desert and arrived. I placed one hand around the back of her neck and let my fingers finally slide into her soft hair. She smelled like vanilla, and a bunch of other fragrances I was too young to identify. I moved closer. She placed one arm on my shoulder. The electricity of her touch sent shock-waves through my defenceless body. Her lips were only inches from mine. So close, I could almost taste her. And this was roughly where one big-ass star took a dump out of the cosmic alignment.

You see, I was a pretty immature teenager. In my sexual development, I was still only at, what I call, the fourth-grade kiss; closed, pouty lips. Kiss-on-the-cheek kind of lips. Sabina was way beyond that. She was well into the tongue kissing. So, our instinctive expectations for the kiss were not aligned. I went in for the closed-lips kiss. She went in for the open mouth kiss, and the catastrophic result was me kissing her... INSIDE her mouth. I still remember the apocalyptic feeling of failure, as the kiss provided nothing of the expected splendour. Destiny had failed me. As soon as I noticed my gigantic mistake, I went in for a second try, but the moment had passed, and I had missed it. I MISSED IT!!! I sat down in despair, as the game went on, and thought of nothing but the goddess and the pre-destined love now forever wasted, as I could never seek such an opportunity on my own. She never fell in love with me.

Strangely, for why should anyone care for failure such as I, we remained friends, and a couple of years later, after we had graduated college, we had spent the night with a few friends at a gay karaoke bar (don't ask) somewhere in Copenhagen. In the end, she walked me out of the bar to say goodbye. I was moving to Sweden to start Performing Arts school, and I knew it would be a long time before I would get a chance to see her again. Maybe I would be all grown up, mature and worthy of her, if that ever happened. I had nothing to lose, so I told her she was the love of my life up to that point. She hugged me. I walked home through the warm Copenhagen night and never saw her again.

Why did I tell you this story? Well, what do you think? In which speech, could this story serve a purpose? What could be the message of this story? I have actually never used this story on stage. I have used it for workshop exercises, for other reasons. This story, how embarrassing as it was at the time, is now my favourite moment. My favourite memory. That late night hug outside the gay karaoke bar would not be as cherished a memory, was it not for the catastrophic kiss years before. If I were to use it, it would be in a talk where the message was something like this:

"Your worst and most embarrassing moments, will sooner or later turn into your most treasured memories."

And the point would be:

"It gets a lot easier to deal with difficult or embarrassing moments in life, as you are in the middle of them, if you can learn to see the positive potential of the future experience gained, while you are still in the moment."

If that was what I was asked to talk about, and I used that story as the middle pathos of my speech, I would have everyone on my side at the end. I would have everyone eating out of the palm of my hand, because it's a story everyone can identify with.

The science of storytelling

There's actually some science to storytelling as well. Because the sharing of stories is the oldest form of communication. It's also rooted in the oldest part of our brain and thus has the strongest emotional impact on us. This is because a whole range of chemical reactions are released into our body depending on the type of story. There are six major chemicals, which cause emotional reactions. Three positive ones and three negative ones. The positive ones are Dopamine, which causes focus, motivation and memory. Oxytocin causes generosity, trust and bonding. Finally, endorphins are released by laughter and causes creativity and focus among others. Let's forget the bad ones and assume that we won't need them. For more on the science of storytelling, I refer to David JP Philips.

The Sabina story is a simple example of an Oxytocin generating story. Oxytocin is also called the Love-chemical, as it's triggered by empathy. The Sabina story very much relies on you, feeling empathy for me at my moment of catastrophe. Oxytocin makes the audience feel love for the speaker which brings me to the ultimate argument for the importance of the personal story.

One very important fact about the story remains, which has been proved by multiple different studies.

"The more emotionally invested people get, the less critical they get." - *J.P. Philips*

If you can get your audience emotionally invested in your story, then by the time you get to your ending, they will think anything coming out of your mouth makes sense. They will want to buy whatever you are selling.

The ending
The logos/the message

If you crafted the opening with care and diligence, and your middle was as emotionally engaging as the story of Sabina, then your ending should be pretty smooth sailing. Just take it home. That is, if you have actually thought out exactly what you wanted to say, and not got swept up in the motivation to change the world for all future generations with one speech. Do not have five different points for a ten-minute speech. Make up your mind.

What you may consider is to memorise the last two sentences of your speech, just as it's advisable to do with your first couple of sentences. Put as much thought and diligence into the last two sentences, as you did with the opening, and really nail that ending. When I say, "nail the ending", I mean neither a misplaced comment on potential sexual preference, nor you, writing something that just sounds as epic, dramatic and linguistically awesome as possible, intending only to impress and inspire. Write accurately and personally what you wanted to communicate. What exactly is your message, and what do you want them to take away that is of value to them?

There is another little known reason why memorising the first sentence of your speech as well as the last sentence is worthwhile. Maybe not a little known, but often overlooked yet incredibly important factor: You have to know what your very first word is and what your very last word is. This not for the sake of the word, but because you have to communicate to the audience exactly when you have started; when they should shut up and pay attention. Likewise, you must tell them indirectly but exactly when your speech is over; when they're allowed to stand up and applaud furiously. The last is by far the most important. In the beginning, if you're any skilled at all, you WILL get their attention, eventually. However, if you don't communicate precisely when you end, you can drop everything you have built up on the floor, and the audience will leave feeling deflated and uninspired, even though what you delivered was good. I have seen this many times at drama-auditions, which is the same as any job-interview. They have their monologue prepared and, in the end, they say the last word, unaware that this is their ending, turn and walk off the floor, leaving the panel with an awkward pause of uncertainty as to whether the aspiring actor has finished or not. The wonderful energy of the otherwise talented performance completely wasted and thrown carelessly on the floor. How could you? You are the captain of the ship, and you must tell the audience exactly when the ship has docked, and it's time to applaud and leave. Know what your first word is and what is your last.

Call to action is the most classic tool to end a speech. If you invite the audience to take action on some level, following the speech, it gives the audience an encouraging sense that there is something they can do too. They too can contribute, both to the better of the world and their own individual lives.

Can I give an example of a good ending, you say? Good question. You're such a clever and astute student. I don't know if I can, because as per usual the suckiness (yes, it's a word, according to the rules I have just made up) of this whole endeavour is that we can never give guaranteed tools, as it all comes down to personal taste. But the obvious thing to do is to go back in time and give you the ending to that story about Mr Free Speech, whom you were dying to hear the fate of earlier.

Example of an ending:

"I can only hope that a Phoenix will rise from his (Free Speech's) ashes and a new place for curiosity will emerge. Because without curiosity, conversation, knowledge, history and the liberty to ask the difficult questions... where will we be?

May he rest in peaceful discussion. Thank you."
- *Martin Svaneborg*

Again, let me break down what we did here:

- First, the mythical creature of the Phoenix is deliberately used to further personify the eternal immortality of free speech in a similar archetypal way, as I did in the opening. The Phoenix is a bird that dies after a given lifespan by bursting into flames, but is immediately reborn from its own ashes, and thus is an indistinguishable flame of light and life. Also, the Phoenix was used in an incredibly successful series of books about a certain underage wizard, so the use of the Phoenix has a strong pop culture reference at present. Finally, with the Phoenix, because it will inevitably be reborn, the metaphor serves as a beacon of hope to the audience that if free speech is indeed like the phoenix, then rest assured, the impending doom will not be eternal.
- Second, we draw on the vastness of time with the sentence: *without curiosity, conversation, knowledge, history and the liberty to ask the difficult questions... where will we be?* Reminding us that free speech has impacted us through centuries on many levels, from curiosity to our very history, and even concerning our freedom to have an opinion. This solidifies the significance and the potential ramifications of the death of free speech. Meaning, this is bloody important.
- Third, by asking: *Where will we be?* I take the message out of just being a strong conviction of mine and laying both the issue and consequences directly into the lives and the hands of the audience.
- Fourth, the call to action: May he rest in peaceful

discussions. It is up to you, the audience, to secure the future of free speech, by holding yourselves true to the integrity of curiosity. It's not unachievable on your part. All it requires is what Jesus proclaimed in Matthew 11:15: He who has ears to hear, let him hear. Meaning, if you have ears, then all it requires to save free speech, is for you to take your individual responsibility in a discussion. Listen! However, if you do not take action in taking part in and promoting the peaceful and open discussion, then you WILL plummet into the prophesied chaos.

With an opening and an ending that achieves as much as these two examples, all that would be needed was a Sabina-like story. Maybe one of my childhood memories growing up with Free Speech as that one friend, whom I could always count on, until he fell sick, a nice little transition about the consequences of Free Speech's death, and that speech would have been knocked out of the ballpark.

17

VENTURING INTO DELIVERY

WE'RE GETTING CLOSE NOW. Can you feel it? It's exciting, isn't it? You have a speech brewing inside of you. Your story. Your voice is waking up from the depths of your soul. You may already have an idea for a super hook of an opening. You remembered that personal story of yours, which could serve to share an important message, and you have a sentence lingering in your mind to end with a bang. How do you prepare it for the stage? If you're not supposed to memorise the whole thing, then exactly what do you do? You visualise your speech! The reason why the campfire type story is so deeply rooted in us, is that those stories work on imagery. Just like my stage story, or the Sabina story, they create images in our heads, and I try to tell them in a way that makes you see the images of the stage or the kiss too. If you remember words, it's usually not because of the impact of the words themselves, but because, when the words were shared with you, they triggered images in your mind, and those images triggered emotions in your nervous system, and your emotions make you remember the words. We can use this to our own advantage when we prepare. It's simply easier to remember an image than a load of text.

***

The map to the treasure

Here's how to memorise a structured speech. You make a physical drawing of your speech. Almost like the map of a treasure hunt. You put your opening up in the right-hand corner, and draw your way around the paper, from the opening, to maybe a first keyword of the topic, to your main story, maybe an intermediate point and one more story, to the ending. Everything is just keywords, with lines and arrows in between pointing from one step to the next. Maybe little stick-figure drawings or smileys along the way to trigger your own memory. At the end, you memorise the first two sentences, know your personal story, memorise the last two sentences, and then you look at your map, and you memorise the image of the map.

I know, you corporate slaves to the digital world will say, "Can't I just write it out like really simple bullet-points?"

NO, you cannot. Because then it is still just words, and you will end up with fifteen bullet-points, meaning fifteen sentences or more, that you have to not only memorise but also remember the order of. You must go into child mode and turn it into a picture. With the drawn map, you're not remembering fifteen bullet-points, you're remembering ONE image, with the entire journey on it. When you do the speech, you will not only remember what the next part of your speech is, but you will also learn to always have a complete internal overview of your speech at all times, so you always know exactly where you are in the speech, should you stumble at any point. If so, you look at your internal map and go: Where was I? You see where you are on the map, like the red *you are here* dot, and see the next step. It's a very powerful way to not only prepare your speech, make it come off as if you have memorised the whole thing, but also be able to jump around or skip parts of your speech if you're running out of time.

You have your speech. You're ready to take to the stage, but before doing that, let's just repeat one phrase from the beginning:

Who is that person you see in the mirror, and who is that person you want to get skilled? How have you become all that you are; the good, the bad and the ugly? You can't expect to get skilled if you're not honest about exactly who that person is in the mirror, whom you now have to deal with in this process.

Are you ready to go up there with all of you; the good, the bad, and the ugly and be honest with it and comfortable with it? I don't mean whether you're unafraid to go up there. We have yet to sort out fear of public speaking. Only two chapters to go before we tackle that one. I mean, are you comfortable going up there being you? Good. Let's make magic.

18

STAGE ANCHORING

The magical sparkle of delivery

I LOVE ANCHORING. I absolutely love anchoring. It's so fun to do on stage, and in my humble opinion the most powerful stage tool to make your speech come alive. That is, as mentioned in the beginning, like with all other tools, if done right. If done wrong, it's just another great way to look like a robot on stage and distract your audience away from an emotional connection.

Anchoring is the cunning use of certain locations on stage. It's also a phenomenon in psychology, where it is dealt with as a cognitive bias, meaning a person receiving a specific piece of information, thus anchoring their mindset and belief on that one piece of information and making all future judgements and decisions based on this information. They are *anchored* in that one piece of information. We can use that to our advantage on stage, playing tricks on the subconscious minds of the audience. Stage anchoring is, similarly, that you choose to be at a certain place on stage, when you deliver a certain piece of information. Then you anchor that piece of information to that place on stage, in the minds of the audience. When you then subsequently return to the place, they will remember both the information given at that place, but more importantly the potential emotional reaction associated with that information. If you take a tour around the landscape of public speaking, go to speaking clubs, look up videos on YouTube, what have you, you will mostly find speakers using anchoring for *time*. However, there are three major ways to use anchoring, and *time* is actually the least powerful of them.

You can use stage-anchoring for the following:

- TIME
- EVENT
- CHARACTER

Anchoring for time. This is the most widely used form of anchoring in the realm of public speaking. If you go to a Toastmasters club or something of the likes, they really like to use time-anchoring. It's the easiest and simplest one to use, but it's also the easiest to use in the wrong way. This might be because of its simplicity. Easy to understand – easy to misunderstand? I'm not quite sure. Anchoring is when you have a timeline running through the narrative of your story, or you jump from one event in time to another. Classic example:

(Speaker starts slightly stage right)

"I was born in a small town. It was a rough childhood, but I guess others have had it worse... (childhood memories)... I walked into the lights."

(Speaker takes a step to the left)

"There I was. First week of college. In front of all the teachers, parents, students, and in front of a microphone... (college memories)... three hours later, the train stopped."

(Speaker takes another step to the side towards stage left)

"As soon as I arrived in Sweden, they turned my world upside down. This was it. It should be awesome, so why was I so lonely..."

You understand the gist of it, right? Every time there is a significant shift in time, the speaker moves to the next spot on the stage, to indicate that that part of the story takes place at that exact spot on the stage, and that spot on the stage becomes a geographical metaphor for that moment in the narrative. Before we go on, let us first just establish exactly why we would want to use anchoring. There are two primary reasons and thus two purposes for using anchoring.

The two intended purposes of anchoring is:

1. **Create subconscious links in the minds of the audience between the space of the stage and narrative to enhance the audience's ability to follow the narrative.**
2. **The enhanced links to the story in the minds of the audience, makes the speaker be able to create stronger emotional responses, because the images created by those links are clearer and more vivid.**

The purposes of the above stage directions are obviously to make the speaker look in control, decisive about the execution of the speech, being in command of the stage, and deliberately helping the audience to follow the speech more clearly. What a noble speaker. But then such a simple task of moving to the left twice falls apart, when the speaker, and I see this all the time, takes an odd stiff step... sideways. Instead of achieving step one towards absolute wizardry shy only of the great Mr Potter, they do the exact opposite and manage what I described in the very beginning as *good intentions gone stupid distractions*. Instead of the audience being wowed by your delivery, they are distracted by your odd display of movement, thinking *why is he walking like a crab?* The reason is, and I know this comes as a complete shock, but HUMANS DO NOT WALK SIDEWAYS! They walk forwards. So, if you take a sudden step sideways across the stage, you do not look human, and the audience can't relate to you as one. Ergo, distraction. If you're practicing this at home, while preparing a speech, and you want to do this, stop when you get to the point of moving to the side. Think. *If I was not conscious about this, then what would have to happen for me to suddenly to move that one step over there?* What is the unconscious thought-process, which triggers me to move to a unique spot, without thinking about it? Think long and hard and try to feel what the natural impulse is to make that happen. What is the thought behind the next sentence that makes you move? It's very subtle, and it's not necessarily easy to replicate an instinctive impulse. Now, turn to the side, take a step forward and turn back to the audience. All in one fluent, human-like subtle movement. Voila.

Anchoring for an event. We're raising the stakes now. It's getting more powerful, but also more delicate, and more of an art form. We're moving into an area, where it's not simply about where you are on stage, but also the thought with which you arrive at a certain place on stage, and the timing between your thought and the stage. *Event* means you can be at a certain place on stage when you talk about a specific event that takes place in your narrative. Then, where you are on stage is not only anchored to the time of the event but also to the emotional impact, the event had on you, the speaker, at the time. Let's take an example right away, so you can follow my train of thought, and as per usual with this author, let's make it a dramatic one:

(Speaker moves to an isolated spot on the stage
otherwise not used in the speech. The speaker stops,
while looking hesitantly down at the floor.
He/she pulls a phone out of the jacket and looks at it.)

"I answered the phone... and that was the moment I found out I had cancer."

If done well, what you achieved is that you have anchored that spot on the floor, in the minds of the audience, as the place where you were diagnosed with cancer. The super powerful tool you now have in your arsenal is, if you later on in the speech are talking about, let's say, how to overcome the fear of conflict, you can suddenly arrive back at that same spot, just when you explain to the audience how to cope with the moment of conflict:

"For years, I had dreaded the moment of conflict. I had foreseen impending doom many times over. Every conversation with my boss. Every wedding invitation I had to turn down. Every conversation with my mom about, why I would not be home for Christmas. Until I realised... I was creating the fear of the conflict myself. It

was me making up a story and expecting a conflict that never turned out as bad as I imagined, anyway."

If you arrive back at that same spot, exactly when you say "realised..." You stop, look down at the floor, pick your phone out of your pocket, look at it and remember that devastating call, look to the audience and say: "I was creating the fear of conflict myself." Then, the audience will know that the source of all your years of fear of conflict stemmed from that one moment, when a moment had the most devastating outcome to you; the moment you were diagnosed with cancer, because now, at the moment of realisation, you are standing in the same spot as the moment of the diagnosis. The audience will put two and two together and understand, not only how your fear of conflict was born but also how to cope with it. So, when you get to your last point and awesome ending, concluding that:

"Fear of conflict is a construct you have created, which stems from a moment in your past, where your worst fears of a conflict were confirmed. Go back and find your moment. Acknowledge that it did not kill you, because you're still here, and every moment since then; every conflict since then has actually been far less of a conflict."

The audience will already know it, and they can just nod in exalted agreement with your closing argument. They will cheer, as you and they have reached an endgame of enhanced enlightenment... together.

Can you see how powerful this stuff potentially is? And we're not done yet.

.   .   .

Anchoring for character. This is the Holy Grail of anchoring. I put the three types of stage anchors in this order, because each of them includes the previous type of anchor as well. You can anchor for time itself. Purely for the sake of easy-to-follow narration. However, you cannot anchor for an event without also creating a link in time to that event. Likewise, you can't anchor for character, meaning a person, without having that character linked to an event which will, in turn, be linked to a time. A character never appears out of thin air, and even if they did, like Jesus before the to-be-apostle Paul on his way to Damascus, that obviously becomes an event in itself. By the way, have you had the thought? Of course, you have, you clever reader, you. What we have with anchoring for character is... wait for it... a trinity of anchoring. See how that title keeps giving?

The reason anchoring for character is the holy grail of anchoring, apart for the trinity part, is that it utilises the people in our story, and as we have earlier established in our look at our history of communication, going back to the campfire story, it's not just about the story, but about the connection between people sharing the stories. You, anchoring for event, can be very efficient, but you, making the characters of your story come to life on stage with you... that will make the audience bond with you on a whole other level. That is where you become a wizard of public speaking.

Instead of me doing a whole lot of explaining, I will give an example instead, and hopefully, like the audience, you will figure it out.

The really interesting story from the beginning of the book, about my debut on stage, is a story I have used many times in different contexts. Do you remember, I have a middle section where I say something like:

"Ten years later, I was at the birthday party of a famous vocal coach, while hovering over the buffet. Suddenly, the director was there."

Right before "Ten years later" I would move to the left side of the stage and anchor the jump in time. I then look down and anchor the event of the party and the buffet, as I take in the look of the shrimps and pawns. I say "Suddenly", turn my head and, in a quick glance, see the director standing next to me. I turn my head back to the audience and say: "the director was there". By that brief look alone, I have anchored the imaginary director who is now standing next to me, and I have the conversation with him that leads to my newfound perspective and subsequent empathy for the man. The last that happens is him saying: "I have never seen a better Emcee before or after you." At that point I leave the director and the anchor, walk out of that part of the narrative, return to the centre of the stage to deliver my conclusion and ending, and here is where the magic happens. In the end, I say something like this:

"So, if in the heat of the moment I say something that hurt or offend you, immediately ask yourself: Do I need to take a stand? And if you do, TAKE IT!... but whatever you do, don't throw away the opportunity to grow and maybe even find your true self in the process. Empathy does not come from choosing to be right or to impress, but choosing... choosing to understand someone's perspective. Choose empathy!"

I'll leave it up to you. What do you think I did in that last pause? YES. I knew I could count on your wit. You are right. After "... impress, but choosing...", I paused for a second, looked over to the left, looked at the director who was still over there by the buffet where I had left him. I looked at him while I said: "choosing to understand someone's perspective." I gave him a slight smile in acknowledgment of the lesson learned. Then I looked back out at the audience and concluded: "Choose empathy!". What had happened? I had spent the entire speech blaming my trials and tribulations on the director, only to, finally, grow up and gain some perspective. The audience had gone with me on that emotional journey being equally frustrated with the director as I had been, and when I finally stopped and looked over, they all knew that *someone*, to me, was the director, and that I had arrived at gratitude of what he had taught me about myself and about life. The whole time span from the nervous breakdown to eventual maturity, the events in between, and the people involved, everything encapsulated in that one anchor, and just one look towards that anchor made the whole story unfold again, making the emotional impact of the final two words increase tenfold. "Choose empathy!" Curtain down. Standing ovations.

Conclusion. With efficient, strategic and well executed anchoring, you enable the audience to fill in the pieces of the puzzle. It makes them feel smart. They will not know why, because it's actually not them being smart, it's you, like a masterful puppeteer, guiding their subconsciousness towards the untold pieces of the puzzle. You enable the audience to feel clever. They will appreciate it and love you for it.

19

WHY NOT VOCAL VARIETY AND WHAT ABOUT BODY LANGUAGE?

Now, we're moving into a few things I would rather avoid all together. This is because they are peripheral factors that may be useful to you but have no real value to your actual skill set or your delivery as a speaker. They're things that you will undoubtedly get acquainted with as called tools, if you roam around speaking communities, but which I call symptomatic attempts at enhancing a speech, when the problem is, in fact, you being a mediocre speaker. And if you want to work with vocal variety or body language, you need extensive awareness into both your vocal cords, and the physical capabilities of your body, and how that translates into an extended language. I could be quite brutal about it and say: If you want to work with vocal variety, go see a vocal coach and learn to sing. You can't work with vocal variety without actual vocal-chord technique. Expect a year or two of training before you have any vocal range worth varying. You can't work with a vocal variety if your vocal range is not more than a major third on the octave scale. If you don't know what that means, then that's my point. If you want to work with body language as a speaker, go talk to your therapist and figure out why you seemingly have none.

Power poses and the chemical reactions produced by such can be of benefit to you, if you need it to boost your own confidence as a speaker. It can also make you come off more competent and thus more authoritative to the audience. But it will not make you a better speaker. There is a great argument to be made for standing up straight, as it will not only make you feel better, but there are millions of years of evolutionary evidence to the effect it has on the people who listen. They will perceive you as a power-figure; one of conviction and authority to whom they will be attracted. It can even enhance your story, as mentioned before, but it will not really make you any better.

If you really want to learn about vocal range and vocal technique, I will refer to Per Bristow. If you really want to work with body language, I will refer to Amy Cuddy.

20

THE ALMIGHTY PAUSE

SPOILERALERT: The one trick above all other tricks to increase your attraction as a speaker comes at the end of this chapter.

Pauses are another celebrated phenomenon in public speaking that I would like to ignore altogether. In my opinion, the pause, in itself, does not exist in public speaking. *But I keep getting feedback that I should use more pause in my speeches.* No, you just need to slow the f... down, temporarily, and pay a little attention to what you're saying. Pauses in themselves, as a public speaking tool, only serves to put your audience to sleep. If that is your strategic objective, then fine. Use a lot of pauses. If you do want a fundamental improvement of your performance level as a speaker, you have to learn to pace. I will talk more about that at the end of the chapter. First, more pause-shaming.

We should only put pauses into a speech deliberately for two reasons. 1) To make listeners, who stopped paying attention, pay attention, and 2) As a natural response to a thought. For instance, the before mentioned example, in the anchoring for character bit, when I stopped at the end and paused to look at the imaginary director, there will be a pause, but it's not for the sake of holding a clever pause. It's because there's a thought. I have to relive my own memory of looking at the director, before my own train of thought arrives at the conclusion, and I can go on. This thought takes a little time, which will create a pause, but the pause is not the thing I am deciding to do. It's just a side effect.

So, forget about the pauses. Just forget it. Devote some time and thought to what you are saying, and which natural thoughts come before each sentence. There is a thought behind every sentence and only one thought. There is a thought behind every memory. There is a thought behind every movement and action you make on stage. The art of the thought behind the sentence is another thing, which actors spend years fine-tuning, exploring the psychological and neurological link between the thought of what to say and the mouth turning it into words; how many words can be generated by one thought, turning the unconscious instinct of thought vs. speech into conscious awareness without losing the feel of spontaneity, et cetera. So, stop believing you can replace all that with the cunning use of a pause or two. Just stop focusing on the pauses. Focusing on pauses would be focusing on when you do not speak. It doesn't make any sense. Focus on when you DO speak and the thought behind it. Focus on what you are saying and why. Period!

BUT… here comes a big, fat *but*. (Yes, I do like big buts, and I just can't lie. Get it? Oooh, my god, I'm so randomly funny. Sorry!)

I happen to be a man of faith. (I know. How about THAT for a segway from big buts?) I have also studied theology. The combination of the two means I have been in many a church, at many a sermon, listening to many a priest. (Disclaimer: This is Denmark. Lutheran Protestant Christian churches) They are public speakers as well, but with a message so powerful, you would think they could have any audience or congregation in the palm of their hand, just from the head-start of their Logos being The Logos. The word of the almighty God. Nonetheless, I have only a few times been truly mesmerised by a priest speaking. I have many times been bored stiff and found myself thinking about anything and everything else but what the preacher was on about. Even though I believe in the faith they preach. Why? Because Danish priests have a strange habit of falling into the one pitfall most unskilled speakers fall into, when trying to be an engaged, passionate speaker. The pitfall is caused by them, in six years at University (4-year Bachelor + 2-year Masters, which is mandatory in Denmark to become a priest – church and state still being linked and all), never receive any training in public speaking. Not one day. Not one single hour of teaching in either communication, rhetoric or performance skills. A fact that still baffles me to no end, considering that the primary job of a priest is what? Right! Communicating a message from a stage through a microphone.

What happens? The pitfall! Which is what? People who don't have any actual skills as a speaker, or knowledge thereof, only have their emotional instinct to go on. So, a speaker with no skills but a lot of good intentions will try to sound really compassionate about the subject. They will talk slower to really make people listen. They will unconsciously add a lot of air (breath) to their voice, because they really caaaaare about the subject. (This one – the breathy voice – is the worst of all. It makes you sound like a completely different person) They will hold pauses to give people time to reflect and be intrigued. All the while, they're sucking the life out of the audience, until everyone is fast asleep from listening to the monotone drone up there. I have often wondered, listening to those kinds of speakers (not priests but speakers in general with a misunderstood conception of what an engaging speaker voice sounds like), what I would say if given the chance. If I got 15 minutes to coach them, what would be the one thing I would change first to make a noticeable change.

The 1 thing that WILL make you better on stage
SPEAKING PACE

TALK FASTER!!! Wow, that was three exclamation marks, and that is as many you're allowed (An English professor once told me, "Never use more than three of anything. It's just vulgar.")

This, ladies and gentlemen, is the one trick above all, which will make you more attractive as a speaker. If you really want people to listen, you don't lower your speaking pace. You don't add a lot of pauses. You speed up! You vary your speaking pace and the energy with which you speak. Things you say have different levels of significance from an emotional point of view. Some things are fact driven and requires at steady pace, clean and concise diction. Some things are sad and require you to slow down and have a feel. Some things are oh, so exciting and require you to speed up and ramble. The common factor is that everything you say has an emotional connection unique to you. You could call it an emotional identity. Everything you say means something to you. Something that might be different to someone else. When you talk, normally, with your friends or family, the pace of your speaking will vary according to the spontaneous energy level of what you're saying. If someone comes through the door, totally excited, they will speed-talk. If they come in scared to say what needs to be said, they will hold pauses and talk slow. The pace of their speaking is guided by the energy of their physical state, and their physical state is governed by their emotions. So, we all have a natural variation in the pace of our communication. This, we can and must use to our advantage as speakers.

BUT. Yes, another great, big but. Here is what most people misunderstand or mis-assume. If you want people to pay attention, DO NOT slow down. The rapid-fire, super-computer that is the human brain is way too sophisticated to be tricked be something so simple as a pause or slow, breathy voice. It's much too advanced for that. It's neuroscience. People who study or practice speed reading know this. If you read a book and A) It takes forever for you to finish the damn thing, and B) when you have read a page, you can't remember any of it. Jim Kwik will then tell you to put some music on and read faster. Much faster. What happens when you read slowly is that your Ferrari of a brain has too much time to think in between the words. Your mind wanders, and you end up not only thinking too much about the words, but about everything else too. What you're going to do later, what's for dinner, et cetera.

The same thing happens to a speaker and to an audience. If you talk with a slow, monotone voice and hold too many pauses, you just enable the listeners to zone out and think about everything else besides you. To get the human brain to pay attention, jolt it and force it to concentrate. You do that by varying your pace and speed up every time you have a legitimate excuse to be excited about what you're saying. Which, hopefully, should be often. Of course, be *in* what you're saying. You have to present. Otherwise, fast pace can lose people too. But if you want the big general tip that works on every speech. Forget about the pause. Think about where you can speed up and fire three sentences at them in one go, without blinking. As if these are the last words they will ever hear, and you are the executioner. Three sentences like a bullet to the head. THEN hold a pause at the end of the firing squad. THAT will wake them up.

21

FEAR OF SPEAKING – A SIMPLE SOLUTION.

OKAY, this is an important one. My experience will suggest there's a really big chance you've been waiting for this very chapter. Fear of speaking, especially in public, is a very legitimate problem, and you should not in any way feel bad, embarrassed or ashamed of being a slave to this. With that said, it's a completely unnecessary problem, and if you're one of those who have wrestled with this fear for a long time, you have wasted a lot of time on something, which doesn't have to be a problem at all. In fact, it has a simple solution and, surprisingly, can be easily fixed. IF you set your mind to it...

What is fear of speaking?

I have mentioned before that the reason we're so prone to respond to stories is because we process them through the oldest part of our brain. Now, I'm not an expert on neuroscience, so this is just a rough sketch. We have an ancient center of our brain comprising multiple small organs like the thalamus, hypothalamus, amygdala, et cetera. All our sensory impressions; what we see, hear, feel, taste, et cetera, goes into this ancient part of our brain, and from there the information is distributed into the big cerebral cortex, which is the big outside part that looks like cauliflower. The cortex, I guess you could call the thinking part, or our intellectual part that decides what to do with the information if we think about it a little. However, we're not programmed to think about it a little. From an evolutionary point of view, we're not meant, primarily, to be intellectual beings. We're programmed to be surviving beings. The personal story goes directly into the ancient part of our brain, because, if told well, it triggers images in our minds, and thus it becomes a sensory experience. That is also why stories have those immediate chemical responses before we can even think about it. Fear of speaking results from the same phenomenon. Because we're built for survival, the ancient part of our brain needs to come up with a story about a future event to determine whether it will be a potentially life-threatening one. If you do not, at the time of deciding to do a public speech, also create a story about how this event will unfold, then the ancient part of your brain, we could also call it subconsciousness (though it's not necessarily the same), will come up with a story of the outcome of the speech for you. AND because your ancient brain is primarily concerned with survival, it will always... as in ALWAYS come up with a worst-case scenario. This means, if you don't correct it, consciously, your ancient brain will go with *this will probably kill you. How do we avoid that?* This, to the point where your entire body will go into full-on defence mode, feverish shakes, anxiety attacks, loss of voice, the whole nine yards. All of it simply because you did not tell yourself any different.

How to cure fear of speaking.

The overall answer to the cure, I have just given you above. Tell yourself a positive story to replace the apocalyptic bad one your ancient survival brain will otherwise generate for you automatically. You also have to be persistent enough with this alternate story to make it the new default setting for you every time you have to speak.

Here's what you do. As soon as you decide to do the speech/talk/presentation/pitch/what have you, then you first have to decide, as mentioned earlier, on your why. What do you want the listeners to take away? When you know exactly what it is you want to communicate to them, then you close your eyes. You imagine the best-case scenario, where the audience reacts exactly how you want them to react. With your eyes closed, see their faces of delight and excitement at what you have just shared with them. Hear their applause, listen to their words of appreciation after-wards. Take the complete experience and all the positive impressions in. Let the impressions simmer for a while and just bask in the glory of the moment. When you open your eyes, you compose your speech to fit that reaction. Once you have your speech ready, then every day, for a week leading up to the day of the event, before you practise the speech, you close your eyes and run that inner video of the best-case scenario. It's even better if you can build on it every time you practise. What you're doing is building a mental highway which will become a new habit to replace the old habit of flight. You build that new highway, by repeatedly giving your nervous system an alternate experience, to what it would otherwise refer to. You see, when you get on stage, it's your voice and your body that delivers the speech, but your voice and your entire body, for that matter, is nothing but a response tool. It's a slave to your brain and your nervous system, and a very loyal one at that. So, if you have allowed your old brain to communicate to your body for a week: *get ready to die*. Then your body will go on stage and do just that. Die! If you, on the other hand, have spent a week encoding a successful outcome into your body, then it will go on stage and do that. No questions asked.

Then I have to address one thing which you will otherwise come running back to me with, as soon as you try this out, which is the thundering statement:

"But I get so nervous that I can't even think straight. I tried to do what you said, but on the day, I was nervous anyway, and it freaked me out."

Nervousness is a good thing. You are supposed to be nervous. Otherwise, you're dead.

Nervousness and excitement are the same thing, and neither of them have anything to do with your fear of speaking or the horror story your ancient brain is conjuring up for lack of your participation. Nervousness and excitement are both just physical states, and they are in fact the same physical state, but interpreted by you as either positive or negative. If you think about a time where you've been respectively nervous and excited and try to analyse how that physically felt in your body. You will conclude that physically it felt the same. The difference was only how you reacted emotionally to that physical state. If you interpret that physical sensation as something bad, you call it nervous. If you interpret it as being something good, you call it excited. Either way, the point is, it's just a physical state, which is fully legitimate in the situation, as you are undertaking something that is unfamiliar and likely uncomfortable to you. The only terrible thing is if you feel neither. Then you're in trouble, because that means you simply don't care, and have no place being up there.

In a workplace, you can start out doing presentations where you initially feel nervous. Later on, you get to a point where you're just not that excited or inspired about getting up there. It can feel like you don't care, but often it's because you've grown indifferent. You've done too many presentations with too little impact, and it doesn't motivate you anymore. If that's the case, then do something next time to deliberately make yourself nervous and jittery. Have you ever experienced your hands randomly shake and feeling like *shit! How do I hide that? How do I control that?* Don't! It's fine. It means you are switched on. I still get shaky hands sometimes after 20 years in front of audiences. Depending on the situation, sometimes I just shove the hand in my pocket, but you don't have to. Show them your shaky hand and say: *See how excited I am about this? My hands are shaking.* And even if you don't mention it, always react to the shakes with gratitude and positivity. Feeling nervous is great. It means you're alive, and your whole system is switched on. It's not a sign that your mental preparation about the positive outcome has failed. The opposite will. When you're up there, standing in the wings looking at your boss, or whoever is in there on stage introducing you, you're playing the inner video of the perfect outcome; the crowd going wild, and the last thing that happens is that you go:

"Wait, where are the butterflies and the jitters? Oh, there they are."

Good. NOW you're ready!

ACT 3

THE HOLY SPIRIT

22

THE PURPOSE OF SPIRIT

HE LOOKED UP IN BEWILDERMENT. "But how is the spirit different from the father and the son?"

The stiffness of the chair strained against the teacher's aging back. There was an oddly empty yet intense glow in the teacher's eyes, as he stared into blank space.

"It isn't."

"And what is the spirit, really?"

"I don't know."

"What?"

"You're not supposed to know."

"I don't get it…?"

For once, the teacher turned and looked at the curious student with mildness.

"Good. You're not supposed to get it. The spirit is a mystery. You are not supposed to understand it. If you believe you have understood it, you can safely assume that you have misunderstood it."

The teacher winked. The curious one became the puzzled one.

. . .

The Christian Trinity and the definition of the spirit, as we know it today, is a fourth century invention. The spirit itself is an ancient concept which is part of the oldest stories and myths of the old testament. Even the very beginning of the bible features the spirit right out of the gates, as what existed even before God sprang into action, with his impressive creation scheme; an already existing spirit, hovering over a dark void of chaos. Just longing for the God part to get his act together.

For centuries after Jesus, the Nazarene had died on the cross, there was an ongoing debate about how to describe and define the divine constellation of this man, who seemed to be Christ, with not only God but the spirit already described in much older scripture. What was this trinity all about, and how did these three entities relate to one another?

In a society, and thus mindset 2000 years older than the one we live in now, you can imagine the arguments could be creative to put it mildly. It was a period where politics and religious belief were one and the same. Sorting out matters of belief was of utmost importance. The concept of the trinity evolved through various stages until it reached a pivotal climax of conflict in the fourth century. Two opposing interpretations of the trinity were ultimately duelling for the win at an all-out Christian show-down in the year 325AD. The Divinity Battle a.k.a. The Council of Nicea. You would think that such a showdown was happening in Rome, the seat of the pope and the Catholic church, but no. The main conflict played out in Alexandria, Egypt. Yes, the city of enlightenment once founded by Aristotle's outstanding student, Alexander the Great. The Roman emperor at the time, Constantine resided in Rome, but had settled on creating the new capital of Constantinople (now Istanbul, Turkey), close to the holy land, to establish a more central location for the control of trading in and out of the

East. However, Alexandria, also part of the Roman empire, had become the epicentre for theology, writing and science. Several of the most influential theological scholars were in Alexandria, and many of the texts later influencing the future of Christianity were written in Alexandria. Here, an elderly bishop, Alexander (No, not the great one. Just a popular name at the time) held the view accepted in the empire, that God and the Son were equal in being god. God was god. The Son was god. Both god and both almighty. Then came Arius, the defiant student of Alexander of Alexandria, and objected. Arius was James Dean in the Alexandrian edition of *Rebel Without A Cause*. But with a cause. He said: "Wait. If both God and the Son are god, then we have two gods, and thus we're no better than those god-forsaken Romans with their multiple pagan gods." Christianity is a monotheistic religion. There is only one true God. If God is god, and Jesus is God, then there is more than one. Slightly confusing? Well, you can see why it took them a few hundred years to get these issues sorted out. Constantine got fed up with all the ruckus. He didn't really care that much, he just wanted order in his empire. So, he called to a trinity-battle in a minor town called Nicea outside of Constantinople and ordered more than three-hundred bishops to show up and not leave until they had agreed on one creed. The debate basically boiled down to this:

Are God and Jesus equally divine; on par with each other? Or is Jesus subordinate in his divinity to God?

I guess you could say, well, who cares? But it really is a fascinating question, because it has roots growing into a need for spirit; a need for understanding what it all means, but more importantly what we, people, are going to use it for in our daily life, so we can be happier and experience more meaning in our lives. Us, pondering manically how to sort out a distinction between the divinity of a God and a Son really is about us displaying spirit. Isn't it? If you take the word spirit out of the religious context, and someone says about someone else: *Wow, she really has some spirit.* It doesn't mean she's possessed by the Holy Spirit. It means she's decisive. She has enough faith in what she does to take action on it. She has a purpose.

I guess you could describe the spirit as that energy existing in everything, even before it was manifested into a father and a son. There's an old Hebrew word for this spirit or energy in the old testament called *Ruakh*. It describes the energy which makes everything happen; what makes you get up in the morning. What makes the wind blow, the trees sway, the leaves rustle and life flow through you. I like to look at the spirit as the purpose of it all. Why do we get up in the morning? Why do we care if the wind blows? Why do we love? Why do we bother talking to each other? What is the purpose with which everything happens? If we have a purpose that serves not only ourselves but the energy and world that surrounds us, then there is spirit.

GET YOUR PURPOSE STRAIGHT

IN PUBLIC SPEAKING, we can compare the holy spirit to the purpose of the message. The spirit and the need for a message. The purpose of why you communicate what you choose to communicate.

If I go back to my really good story from act 1, then there's a purpose for why I would want to share that story. There are several points and arguments to the story: 1) That I wanted to give him (the director) what he wanted once I understood his perspective. 2) Setting someone up for defeat at every attempt does not make you stronger. That is mental terror and will break you. 3) I could have solved my frustrations back then, if I had known how to have the conversation. 4) With empathy, you cannot only understand a perspective other than your own but also enable your own growth. Several points. However, there can only be one overall purpose to getting on stage and making your voice heard. Either you are there to serve or be served. Either you are there to help or find help. Either you are there to see or be seen. You need to get your purpose straight.

The dangers of social media and the dangers of us

diverting away from face-to-face communication to only written communication (yes, I get the irony of me writing a book about it) is not only inhibiting our ability to grow in ourselves or find meaning in this world. It's also directly eroding everything we stand on. Our societies. Our democracies. Our families and our relationships. If we shy away from face-to-face conversation, and we allow ourselves to disintegrate into an ever-crumbling lack of communication skills, then we're not getting any closer to that magical catch phrase that you have all heard and love. *Change the World.* How many times have you heard that phrase? With a very serious and ambitious intent, I might add. In speeches, movies, Instagram memes, Facebook posts, hashtags, videos, photos and conversations. Yet, if you think about all those people, me included, who claim they want to change the world, obviously for the better, how often has that happened? How many times has anyone changed the WORLD? *If we stand together, we can change the world.* How often has a large group of people joined forces and actually changed the world? I would say never. In fact, I can think of two changes of paradigm shift-level proportions, where I would say the world changed for the better, and they were both accomplished by singular individuals. The first one was Jesus of Nazareth and the second was Nikolaus Kopernikus (Copernicus). Possibly a third being Johannes Gutenberg. Don't misunderstand me and think I, by Jesus, mean Christianity or The Catholic church, which ended up being an awe-inspiring study in corruption and greed. I mean the man from Nazareth. That dude, who could inspire those around him so much that minds were shifted, and art, culture and societies were created. One man's message of love that ended up eroding the tyranny of the Roman Empire as well as the idea of slavery and ultimately founded the entire western civilised world. The second one, Kopernikus, changed the world completely by establishing that Earth was not the centre of the universe, but actually revolved around the sun. Until then, human mind and all its achievements had been related to on the premise that we humans could decide for ourselves, how the world was created, based on our subjective belief. Kopernikus gave humanity a huge slap in the face and served a lesson in humility of divine proportions. He single-handedly forced the world and humankind to rethink everything. Everything we had established as facts, and which we had built our societies on, suddenly crumbled like sand through our fingers. All the figures of power; popes, emperors, kings, the lot of them had to succumb to the fact that they were not the masters of the universe. They too could be wrong. Not just a little wrong, but catastrophically, apocalyptically wrong. Priests, bishops, scientists, philosophers, teachers, everyone had to start over from scratch in a new world based on the humiliating fact: We do not know everything, and we are not the centre of the universe. Speaking of knowing, do you remember Aristotle's master, Plato? Plato wrote the accounts of his master, Socrates, and guess what Socrates had stated 2000 years before the greed of humanity had decided otherwise? "The only thing I know is that I know nothing."

Are we changing the world? No. Are we even getting closer? No. Can we change the world? No. So, why bother? Because we have spirit. We're all creatures of faith. We all believe in something. Even the atheists have an adamant belief that there is no God, and those who believe so are suckers. It's an impressive belief. We can't help ourselves. We're flawed little humans who need something to do. We must have a purpose.

24

THE DANGER OF POLITICAL
CORRECTNESS

THE NEXT COUPLE of chapters may leave you slightly confused unless I state my intent first. The following addresses some of the most important issues, in my mind, plaguing our society these days. Issues like political correctness, gender and identity politics, flirting, sexism, addiction to social media, et cetera. It will get somewhat philosophical from here on out to the point, where you may end up going: *I thought this was a book about public speaking? Why are we talking about flirting?* It is about public speaking, but I believe that our competence for public speaking should take a far greater responsibility than it does now, where it is primarily a business or entertainment tool. In my opinion, a lot of these issues are not getting solved, because there seems to be an underlying problem with communication. It seems like we don't come up with any really viable solutions to any of the problems, because we can't agree on what the nature of the problems are. Meaning, we don't know how to discuss the issues because we are either not competent enough speakers or can't agree on a mode for or premise of communication for any of the issues. So, I bring these coming issues into this book, because they are incentives for why we should become better speakers. So, we can talk about these sensitive issues in a more constructive way. The alternative is not only a lack of discussion but a fuel for division and hate between us. Let's start with one of my favourite issues.

Thus, it's time for me to get on my soapbox and go into full preacher-mode.

Political correctness is a polemic issue to address, and one that I am wary of venturing into in a book like this, where I can't go into the full depth the issue deserves and require. I could write a whole book about this issue itself, but in this book, being not just a tutorial guideline to becoming a more proficient speaker, but also a philosophical view on why it's important for us, not just to speak at a more competent level, but also be aware of the purpose with which we do so, I have to address this issue. Because why should we become better at speaking and communicating if we're not allowed to? And that is where we are heading.

This is my personal creed of faith:

Speak your mind under the assumption that you will offend. If you do not offend anyone, then what you have to say is not important enough.

I believe that one of the biggest dangers to our modern society today is political correctness. With all its good intentions, it is failing catastrophically, and we're all suffering as a result. No one wins. No one is saved. No one is uplifted. Just like my wonderful philosophical speaker-friend, staring into the abyss of lost emotional control, not being afraid to take the plunge, so too are we all, humanity, collectively standing on the edge, staring into the abyss of chaos. But we're not prepared for the plunge, and we should be afraid. Terrified. Because behind us is a bunch of people progressively advocating political correctness, while pushing all of us closer to the edge, like the Pied Piper of Hamelin who played to the rats so seductively that they followed him without questions to the edge of the cliff until they had all gone over, and he was the only one left on the edge. So too are certain groups playing the Siren song of PC under the veil of a moral high ground. Why is political correctness an issue of such implications and potential mayhem? Because we either have political correctness or the freedom of speech. We can't have both. Freedom of speech is the bedrock of our civilised world. It is our democracy on which our societies, our jobs, our lives, our identities within this world rests. Why is it either or? Because political correctness has become a game not of, *you should be considerate of your language to try to understand the person next to you*, but a game of, *you can't say that about the person next to you, because they may get offended, or even worse, I may get offended on their behalf.*

Don't get me wrong with what I am about to say. Too many have abused freedom of speech deliberately to mock and ridicule certain groups. But out of that has risen a self-proclaimed defender of the weak called *political correctness,* and the defenders tend to be people who do not belong to any of the minorities they claim to defend. But who are they to assume, let's say, gay men are weak and need to be defended? Who are they to judge that women are weak, have been oppressed and need to be defended from patriarchy? There are beautiful examples popping up daily of women showing with dignity, integrity and decisiveness that they can stand up for themselves. They don't need us men to be offended on their behalf. They just need to be heard, acknowledged and respected for their vocalisation of free speech, so we can change an aspect of society that clearly has room for improvement. They don't need political correctness. They don't need anyone to be offended. They need someone to listen. Someone to speak. Someone to understand. They need respect, and they need to heal.

There are laws in place, in almost every major country in the civilised world about what you can't say, and that's fine, because of course there are malevolent people out there who speak hurtfully out of ill will, and their actions must be punishable. But legislation is now creeping in major countries otherwise founded on principles like freedom and liberty for all, not about what we can't say, but what we have to say. That is a slippery slope so easily exploited to inhibit people from being allowed to state their opinion or ask an honest question.

Two of the hot topics within political correctness, in recent years, have been racism and gender pronouns. I'm not going to write about racism, because I think there's such a self-evident solution to it. Let me ask your opinion. What will work best to eradicate racism: To lock someone up in jail who utters hateful speech about someone's race or ethnicity, so they can continue the scheming of their malicious ideologies hidden away from the public, or let them speak, yell and shout out in the open for maybe several years, until the public eventually decides if it's a route that has served them any good, or they have had enough and will choose a different path? As the Scottish comedian, Daniel Sloss, remarked, *in my country we have free-range stupidity.* Such has an enormous self-regulating effect. To me, it's a no-brainer.

The discussion of gender pronouns has also suffered tremendously under the impact of political correctness, as there are questions unasked due to the fear of offense. Questions that need to be asked and answered for understanding to be achieved. However, I can't even venture into this respectfully without trailing too far off the path of our overall subject here. So, I will leave the subject for now with this:

It's impossible to talk about difficult things and get important messages out while offending no one. It must be okay to offend as we stumble awkwardly but valiantly in an imperfect attempt to talk about that which is difficult. It's not okay to deliberately hurt or slander other people's race, religion, gender identity, et cetera... but it must be okay to offend if it comes from a source of curiosity with an honest wish to understand a perspective other than your own.

25

IF THEY CALL YOU AN ASSHOLE,
THEY ARE RIGHT.

THE GREAT AMERICAN PHILOSOPHER, Louis CK said: *If someone says you're an asshole, you don't get to decide that you're not.*

Professor Bruce Pardy, in a debate with Dr Jordan Peterson, noted that there is a strange phenomenon going around now, where many people cling to the ideology that *the world is obligated to validate your view of yourself.* I have seen this many times in my years in theatre, which is an industry filled with narcissistic eccentrics longing for validation and attention. I was one of them. It never works out well for the one insisting on receiving the validation. It would have killed me had I not wised up. The ones who end up thriving in showbiz are the ones who can take criticism, but more importantly the ones who can learn to accept that others may view you differently than you view yourself. Showbiz is a world of typecasting, and I have, several times, at auditions for some show been cut after the first round. Such a hit to your vanity can easily make you go: *what the hell? I was the best one there. How can they cut me after the first round?* Well, they can because that's their job. In the beginning I got all offended and vain, but thankfully, I learned that there were many factors playing into me landing the part. Fail just one factor, and you're out. Maybe I was the best one there, but often that was not the determining factor. I was more likely just not the right type for the job. Much more interestingly though, it could be, much to the disagreement of my view of my splendid self, that the choreographer or director found me arrogant and maybe a little too full of myself. I have seen several people lose out to the otherwise wonderful world of showbiz, ending up bitter and resentful, because they would not accept that people around them viewed them differently than they did.

What kind of friend would I be, if I just blindly and obligingly validate your view of your own identity, if you're actually behaving like a narcissistic egomaniac, and quite frankly are being an asshole? If your view of yourself is slowly but surely destroying your life, and you've not seen the clues yet, then me complying to validate you is not only morally corrupt on my part but hurtful to you. In the words of Jordan Peterson: *How do you know if the identity you have decided on is good for you? You are too complex to know that.* You, insisting on me having to describe you as you please, and not being allowed to offend you, will not do you any good. Quite the contrary. This is the danger of political correctness. It's promoted under a false pretense of being able to solve a problem it will only enhance. It does not serve its intended purpose. Political correctness simply does not work.

The beauty of offending

The most beautiful benefit of communication and our incredible invention of language is the ability it gives us to understand each other better. If we're never offended, we're never forced to look outside the tiny box of our already defined opinions and view of the world. Every time we're offended, we are forced to think, and thinking is an incredibly difficult and complex thing to do. We need help to think. We need to get offended once in a while. The most beautiful gift you give someone is to offend them involuntarily. I will say it again:

It must be ok to offend if it comes from a source of curiosity with an honest wish to understand a perspective other than your own.

26

FLIRTING – A DYING ART OF COMMUNICATION

ONCE UPON A TIME in a beautiful town called Verona, there was a boy who fell head over heels in love with this girl he met at a party. They were from rivalling families, the Montagues and the Capulets. The families despised each other, so an introduction was highly flammable. But he did not care. He just walked right over to her, and in a flood of exuberantly flirtatious phrases told her how hot she was. Oddly enough, this brash, inappropriate declaration of attraction did not offend her. She was intimated, yet charmed. Of course, she did not respond immediately to his bold move, as it was delivered in such an out of context, weird and unexpected manner. He continued to stalk her day and night, lurking around her forecourt, hiding from the exposing light of the moon. Even hiding under her balcony. When she noticed his stalky behaviour, she was, surprisingly enough, not appalled. Quite the contrary. She took well to it and invited him to continue his stalky behaviour, which so many others should have been disgusted by and maybe even compelled to report to proper authorities, so the insolent youngster could have been thrown into a correctional facility befitting of his disgusting behaviour. The reason for her completely unreasonable acceptance of his behaviour was very simple. She was interested.

Sexism is another scorching hot topic in recent years. Since the launch of the #Metoo movement by Tarana Burke back in 2006, with the goal of providing a chance for healing to victims of sexual abuse and sexual harassment by enabling victims to speak up, it exploded in 2017 with the exposure of a certain American film-producer. Since then, the fight against sexism has blazed on, but the healing part has got somewhat lost in the short-term, superficially gratifying achievement of judgement and eternal punishment. I am all for the #Metoo movement in Tarana Burke's original form, but much to my sadness, we're seeing accidental, innocent casualties in the war against sexism. One innocent soldier, lying wounded and dying by the wayside, is the flirt.

DISCLAIMER: Let me just repeat why I put these seemingly random topics here in the third act of our journey. It's to put our ability to speak competently into various contexts of communication to see how our choice of communication affects us now, as opposed to how we have dealt with the implications of communication in the past. You see, I don't think we're moving forward with our choices for communication. So, let me just make a bold statement about flirting, which I hope will incite discussion:

Flirting is only viewed as inappropriate, if the person at the receiving end is not interested. Then it is called sexism.

If you, by any chance, should feel yourself getting angry at the above, know this: You may be getting angry because you assume that I endorse sexual harassment. I don't. Flirting and sexual harassment is not the same. Flirting has become frowned upon as a casualty in the rightful fight against sexual harassment. The potential loss of flirting is something I could easily disregard as a triviality of no major consequence to our overall topic of public speaking and our purpose for communication. I think it's more important than that, though.

To advocate the argument that it should always be healthy and acceptable to flirt in any situation, we must first identify very clearly what flirting is, but more importantly, what flirting is definitely not. Flirting is not sex. Flirting is not an invitation to sex. Flirting is not dating. Flirting is not an invitation to dating. Using or abusing a higher position of power in a hierarchy, being a film producer, a boss, a director, a teacher, et cetera, to persuade your way to sex is not flirting. It's a morally degrading act. Abusing a higher position of power in a hierarchy, being a film producer, a boss, a director, a teacher, et cetera, to force your way to sex, or being anybody simply forcing their way to sex is not flirting. It is rape and is punishable by law. Flirting and sexual harassment are not the same. Sexual harassment is an act of sexual attraction imposed upon others in a workplace, professional, or social situation. It is what you do. I am not talking about how you should act or behave. So, I'm not talking about the hand on the back, or the slap on the ass, or the caressing of hair, or the stealing of a kiss. Or worse. I'm just talking about what we should be able to say to each other. You can see flirting as the freedom of speech aspect of political correctness.

Flirting, in itself, is simply a compliment and the purest display of attraction. Something that any man should be not only allowed but called to do with any woman he finds attractive in any kind of way and vice versa; any woman should be free to flirt with a man anywhere, without being assumed a sexist predator. The dictionary definition of flirting is: *To behave as if sexually attracted to someone, although not seriously.* NOT seriously. Sexual harassment is with intent. Flirting is without. This definition causes for such wonderful uses of the word as "On the other, however, the opera and its surrounding texts carefully evade the conse-quences of such flirting." - Cambridge English Corpus. Language can be so beautiful.

Let's go back to how my experience suggests most people define flirting as being an invitation to dating or sex. Where does the balance of power lie in a dating situation? With the woman. The woman owns the power of choice in dating. She is the selector for that simple reason that she, evolution wise, is the baby bearing side of the equation. She gets to choose whose baby she will bear. Yes, women, you have the power. I know many women will struggle to believe this, but it is the truth. Women own dating. It's the man's obligation to make his attraction known to the woman and give her the choice and thus the power. But dating and flirting are not the same, and we should never expect flirting to lead to dating. Dating has no relevance to this book, but flirting does, so, let's keep dating out.

I dare the proposition that no woman will prefer never to be flirted with. They will recline being flirted with in the wrong situation, but what is the wrong situation, and who gets to decide the parameters for the wrong or the right situ-ation. Here comes the bold side-question. How often is *the wrong situation* defined wrong because the one at the receiving end of the flirting is simply not interested? If they WERE interested, would they then judge it as the wrong situation? If the doctor, who flirted with the nurse at the hospital ends up marrying that nurse, and they fall madly in love, will they then tell their grandchildren a story of the wrong situation?

In an ideal world, men should make it a virtue to always flirt under the assumption that women will not be judgmental about their agenda or purpose for flirting. Unfortunately, that's not the state of the world now. We have made a virtue out of judgement. The assumption of motivation behind flirting should never be anything other than a compliment. Flirting is not an invitation for sex. It's not even an invitation for dating. It's simply a statement of unserious attraction, and if you find someone attractive, man, woman or anywhere on the non-binary scale, for that matter, you should make your attraction known, because the world would be a much more pleasant place, with a lot less skepticism and cynicism, if everyone was told everyone once in a while that someone else found them attractive, without feeling required to view the person stating their attraction with immediate contempt.

Without a kind of flirting, found offensive to some, we would not have such literary beauty as Romeo & Juliet.

To tie this back into the art of speaking, if you think about a speaker really having a connection with an audience; the buzz of excitement is palpable in the room. What is happening is that the speaker is flirting with the audience, and they like it. They are interested. It's not flirting in the sexual sense, but the speaker is making sweet love to the audience, in the same way as a movie-actor on fire is making sweet love to the camera, or a jazz-singer is making sweet love to the pianist. If flirting is taken down by a stray bullet in the war against sexism, then we lose our ability to connect. We have to be allowed to flirt.

THE ADDICTION TO SOCIAL MEDIA

MANY YEARS AGO, when I ventured into theatre, I was addicted to attention, and that drove me to the stage. However, it was an addiction which I had spent most of my childhood and teenage years growing and cultivating. These days you can grow an addiction to attention within a matter of months, because there are now technological advancements in place, which works actively and deliberately to make you addicted.

It could be argued that the greatest technological achievement of the past half century is the invention of the internet or the World Wide Web. It could also be argued, because of the internet, that the greatest advancement within communication in the last decades has been the invention of social media. At least that is what most people would take for granted until the last few years, when horrifying studies have shown the opposite. Now, the only really positive thing to be said about social media is the immediacy with which you can communicate. On all other levels, social media is wreaking havoc to humanity and our ability to not only communicate but also define ourselves. Social media were created with a lot of good intentions for how to bring people together. How to share ideas more effectively. How to interact more easily. All to an extent were former CEOs, software designers, programmers, et cetera, are jumping ship and running away from the SoMe-companies like wild horses from a fire.

In 2020, a very disturbing film, The Social Dilemma, arrived on one of the major streaming services, detailing the terrible impact social media is having on our global society, told by the very people who have created the technology. In my opinion, it's one of the most important films to have come out in the last couple of decades. The film links the growing division, racism, hate speech, growing depression and suicide rates, et cetera, directly to social media.

The reason we're all so divided and hatred is filling the world, is that truth does not exist anymore. Well, that's not entirely true. There is one little endangered corner left in the land of the internet, where truth still endures. It's called Wikipedia. A scorned, strange little land, where whenever you ask a question, everyone will get the same answer. But that's not the land we, as human beings of the civilised world, live in anymore. When we watch videos on YouTube, what we believe is truth, is in fact an altered reality that has been tailored and customised by algorithms to your individual preferences, and a personalised truth is formed, where you are constantly confirmed that what you believe is in fact truth, based on your preferences on social media. I know this sounds like a conspiracy theory, but it's not. This is how social media works, and you can't get your message out on social media unless you accept that. As long as we try to live in the world based on the premises of an algorithm, we don't stand a chance.

Most people are of the notion that social media is

drowning us in a flood of posts, pictures, videos and comments. An overload of information, lovingly referred to as the noise of social media. Businesses struggle with this issue, because social media has become the dominant form of advertisement. You can't advertise for anything, without having social media as your primary strategy for advertisement. But it has become so difficult to get a message out and get tangible exposure, because there's too much noise to break through.

Here's my opinion. The noise is not the problem. Our relationship with each other as humans is the problem.

Here are a few statistics from the Social Dilemma. Since the invention of the like-button on Facebook, which was intended to spread positivity, the opposite has happened. We have got addicted to likes. To an appalling extent, where young people now define their own worth by the amount of likes they get for a modified, filtered picture they have posted, not even vaguely resembling their authentic look, anyway. The sole purpose of their existence becomes to get attention from this algorithm. In the United States of America, from 2009 to 2019, hospitalisations because of self-harm (self-cutting, etc.), among girls aged 15-19 had increased by 62%, and among girls aged 10-14 by 189%. Suicides among girls aged 15-19 have increased by 70%, and among girls aged 10-14% by 151%. A 151% more girls aged 10-14 are killing themselves within a decade. That's nothing short of catastrophe. Why are more than twice as many young girls suddenly deciding they're worth so little that death is the better alternative? It's not because kidnapping and sexual assault have more than doubled. Everything points at social media.

This is why, what this book is about, is so bloody important. Why communication, not being a post or a comment on social media, is so important. Social media is not communication. As long as we don't have any greater priorities than likes, we will never grow. The only way to get beyond the algorithms is to be you. Where is your heart? Where is your desire? Where is that story of yours that could make someone else turn away from suicide?

28

DON'T EAT THE BIG WHITE MINT.

I KNOW, I've already quoted a few absolute classics from the world of movies, but probably my favourite quote of all time, is from another cinematic masterpiece. Road House. The wonderful late 80's film starring Patrick Swayze, who plays a legendary bar-bouncer. At some point Swayze's character, Dalton calls his buddy Wade, played by Sam Elliot to ask him how things are at his end, and to find out where Wade is currently working. Wade (Sam Elliot) sums up the description of the bar in which he is also a bouncer with the perfect line:

"This place has a sign over the urinal that says: *Don't eat the big white mint!*"

The bar and the surrounding society, perfectly summed up by one little metaphor. The reason I love that line so much, and it keeps popping up in my mind every now and then, even in the most inappropriate of situations, and then puts a smile on my face, is the duality and scope in such a seemingly trivial little sentence. On the surface, it's a description. There are people in Wade's bar/town, so stupid, they will mistake that white thing lying in the urinal for a treat, when in fact it's there to relieve the stench of piss. But, at the same time, it's the most profound of philosophical statements. Things are not always what they seem. You can look at an object time and time again, having convinced yourself whole-heartedly of the nature of the object, only to be confused when your judgement is clouded, or the spur of a moment, a sudden rush of perspective, can change your perception of the object entirely.

Of greater consequence, alcohol can have the same numbing effect on your mind and your ability to think and reason, as people who are ideologically obsessed. People can become so convinced of the truthfulness in their belief that no argument can provide perspective to them, and their only objective is to convince the rest of the world of the truthfulness of their belief. You can get so caught up in your own belief, if you're never exposed to other opinions or to open conversation; if you're never slightly offended and occasionally have your beliefs gently notched around, then your beliefs are no longer beliefs, because if you only believed then that belief could be changed. But your belief has become an ideological obsession that you treat as a fact. Likewise, but opposite, that shadow of yours; that unconscious world of darkness within us can persuade us of the unmistakable awfulness and ugliness in ourselves. We can convince ourselves that we are worthless, useless, disposable beings with nothing of value to contribute to either ourselves or anyone around us. No one is better at deceiving us than ourselves. This to where, when you think you're eating a delicious white mint, what you're actually eating is a piss-soaked ball of bleached chemicals.

The only way to avoid ideological obsession, which is where political correctness among other topics are heading, is to train and expose yourself to open conversation on a regular basis. And the more skilled the speakers on either side of the conversation are, the more valuable the conversation will be to both parties.

The only way to avoid the all too understandable self-loathing of your entire being – and understandable, as humankind really is a horrendous beast capable of the most despicable acts of free will – is to notch ourselves into the conversation every now and then. Expose ourselves to other people's opinions and the likely terrifying truth that most people don't loathe us as much as we loathe ourselves, or at least should loathe, because we really are awful.

It's not so strange then, with this understandable contempt for ourselves that we take to social media for the wrong reasons, and that we communicate for the wrong reasons. And we do, as the above statistics have shown. Most of what is posted by most people on social media is not with an honest wish to connect and share with friends and loved ones for social reasons. Most posts are motivated by a need to be praised for their attempts to appear as admirable people.

There's this person I know. I used to hang around the same circle with her for a while. She was a lovely and kind person. The best of hearts. I soon noticed this strange, but to me, very obvious duality in her, though. Both her voice and facial expression would change drastically depending on what she was talking about. She had a private person mode, where her voice would be almost childlike. Small, sweet and innocent. Then if she talked about anything from a professional point of view, it was like she had to put on this teacher's hat. Her face changed. Her voice changed. The pace and tone of her voice changed. It was like she felt compelled to come off as someone of a certain level of competence; someone who was the best and most knowledgeable in her field; the one who could contribute incredible value to anyone in her area of expertise. And you might say, well, isn't that completely normal to want to come off as knowledge-able in your area of expertise? Yes, but the change in her was like night and day. Like Jekyll and Hyde. And it takes one to know one. She also happened to be really good at baking. On social media, she would never post anything about herself. However, she would post a ton of pictures of cakes and pastry she had perfectly created, and brought as surprise gifts to her colleagues, and the comment field would flow with praise and thank-yous from the recipients of her baking, with comments of what a wonderful person she was. I had wondered about this charade of perfection, because I thought it was noticeable, and had wanted to ask her about it, if the chance ever presented itself.

One day she suffered a terrible accident and was hospi-talised. Her entire upper body more or less crushed. One evening I went to visit her at the hospital to see if I could get her to open up about this need for coming off like a saint in front of others. It was just me and her alone and a dark, empty, late-night hospital room. To get the conversation going, I told her a bunch of my own childhood memories of abandonment and how it had resulted in addiction to get attention and praise from others. I was sure that this was the root of her behaviour too. She admitted that she never opened up about personal stuff and never wrote anything about herself on social media. She knew it was all cake pictures. However, I never really got her to tell me what I think she needed to tell someone. I don't think many of all her cake-receivers came to see her in the hospital.

I little while later, I spoke to a friend who told me that our common friend had told her of my visit at the hospital. Our bed-written, injured friend had retold the story is if she had shared some personal issues with me, so she could help me talk about my childhood. She had either not understood why I was there or been unwilling to accept the opportunity to talk about something difficult and maybe painful. She would rather remain the one who, even from a hospital bed, was able to be the saving friend who could alleviate someone's need for a talk.

Months later, around Christmas time, I noticed a post she had made. She had decided to cook, for free, for families who were in financial distress, delivering Christmas aid, and asked for recommendations for families, who might be in need of her help. Of course, the comment field again overflowed, not with suggestions of families, but with praise for her inspiring initiative and for the beauty of her as a person. It is speculation on my part, but I don't think any of them ever dared to ask her, as a friend, why she had such a need to come off as a saint.

This is a question that arises in me often these days. The latest craze on the digital platforms seems to be all these people who launch podcasts and vlogs to promote all kinds of wonderful well-wishes for humanity. Self-development. Self-growth. Coaching in finding your inner beauty and strength. Healing. Mindfulness. Love. So many wonderful people with so many wonderful intentions on other people's behalf. So many posts from these do-gooders. So many pictures of them every day on their Instas and what have you, inviting you to let them help you, heal you, guide you, support you, love you and of course like their pictures and write nice comments about their good, Samaritan endeavours. It's not charity, of course, because they do want to charge you money for their help, so they can make a living out for their compassionate nature. I don't claim that their well-wishes are not admirable for the most part. I merely stumble constantly over the ginormous boulder of a question: How much of that quest to help other people in the full blazing spotlight of social media is an honest and pure wish to make other people develop for the better, and how much of it is them having a need for attention and validation, trying to patch together a sense of self-worth they have struggled to maintain earlier on in their lives, by being able to save others? Are they communicating for the right reasons and in the right way?

Jesus said (supposedly):

> "So, when you give to the needy, do not announce it with trumpets, as the hypocrites do in the synagogues and on the streets, to be honoured by others."
> - *Matthew 6:2*

The German philosopher, Immanual Kant was even more staunch about the matter. He was a fascinating case of OCD long before it was a trend with daily routines you could set your clock by. Another really good story. He formulated what is known as the Categorical Imperative:

> "Act only according to that maxim whereby you can, at the same time, will (wish) that it should become a universal law." – *Immanuel Kant.*

In other words: You should behave in such a fashion that all your actions have a moral integrity sufficient to turn every action you make into law, making every behaviour legal and acceptable by all others whereby to act the same way at all times. Everyone should, by law, be allowed to do everything you do at all times in any situation. That's a high barre to set on the infallible ability of humankind.

Concerning morals, he stated that nothing you do for

someone else can be regarded as morally good, if anyone else knows about. In that case, outsiders must assume that you're doing good for selfish reasons, by letting other people know about it, and then it's not only morally bad but corrupt. That's harsh, right? I mean, who can live up to that?

There's too much *look at my face and tell me I am good* and too little content. Too little concern for character. Too little appreciation of character. If you want to be a speaker, you may want to check that mirror again. You may also want to check what the majority of the comments under your posts are about. How are you being judged and, more importantly, WHAT is being judged?

It's a good 50 years ago that Dr Martin Luther King Jr. stated the paramount necessity involved concerning our chance to move forward as a collective human race. *I have a dream that one day my four little children will not be judged by the color of their skin, but by the content of their character.* Nevertheless, judging by the colour of our skin is exactly what's happening in our society today. We're no longer concerned with listening, and hearing what people have to say, but focus on who's saying it, how and why. This is the reason so many private people and corporate businesses alike struggle to get seen and heard in the online jungle of communication, because content is no longer valued. We prioritise appearance and ideology. We're judging each other based on the colour of the skin, while we are unwilling to hear what another person has to say; what the content of their character really is. That is the state of the world, and there's something rotten about it.

To reach someone with your public speaking skills is a monumental task these days. The first is easy. Get skilled as a speaker. You don't have to be a superstar. Just get better. But then comes first a super uncomfortable quest followed by a near impossible quest. The uncomfortable part being you making sure that the content you put out, for all to respond to, is in fact a big white mint and not a piss-soaked ball of bleached chemicals. The near impossible quest: You must then get people to listen. You must make them care about what you say. If you fail to make them listen, then they're still judging you by the colour of your skin and not by the content of your character, and if the colour of someone's skin is more important to us than their character, then we have sadly got nowhere in the last 50 years.

Communicate. Both with yourself and others. Face to face with others. Have conversations, ask questions, be curious, listen, engage, and do not be afraid to be honest.

29

TO BE OR NOT TO BE

WE ARE NEARING the end of my rant and getting to where it is time to make some decisions. If you become a better speaker, what does that mean, and what can you be in the world because of it. It boils down to some very fundamental, philosophical questions. What does *being a better speaker* turn you into? What does it turn your surroundings into? Why is it so important that we don't misunderstand or misuse the concept of communication? I have to turn to one of the absolute titans of literature to shed light on these questions.

"To be, or not to be, that is the question:
Whether 'tis nobler in the mind to suffer
the slings and arrows of outrageous fortune,
or to take arms against a sea of troubles
and by opposing end them.
To die—to sleep, no more; and by a sleep to say
*   we end*
the heart-ache and the thousand natural shocks
that flesh is heir to: 'tis a consummation
devoutly to be wish'd.

To die, to sleep; to sleep, perchance to dream—
    ay, there's the rub:
For in that sleep of death what dreams may come,
when we have shuffled off this mortal coil,
must give us pause—there's the respect
that makes calamity of so long life.
For who would bear the whips and scorns of time,
th'oppressor's wrong, the proud man's contumely,
the pangs of despised love, the law's delay,
the insolence of office, and the spurns
that patient merit of th'unworthy takes,
when he himself might his quietus make
with a bare bodkin? Who would fardels bear,
to grunt and sweat under a weary life,
but that the dread of something after death,
the undiscovere'd country, from whose bourn
no traveller returns, puzzles the will,
and makes us rather bear those ills we have
than fly to others that we know not of?
Thus conscience does make cowards of us all,
and thus the native hue of resolution
is sicklied o'er with the pale cast of thought,
and enterprises of great pitch and moment
with this regard their currents turn awry
And lose the name of action."

"Soliloquy" – Hamlet.

Shakespeare's brilliant question here is: Why is it better to live than to die?

Why do we think it nobler to suffer all the inevitable misery that comes with fortune, rather than just end it all? Why is *being* better than *not being*, when all we do in life is complain and accuse and suffer? A lot of young women and girls certainly seem to think that *not being* is rapidly becoming the preferred. All of life is nothing but calamity, heartache and despised love, the whips and scorn of an oppressed life. Why do we choose that over death? I love the phrase, *when he himself might his quietus make with a bare bodkin* which roughly means, *when we could make ourselves quiet with a knitting-needle.* We could just kill ourselves. Why don't we? Especially if dying is nothing but *to sleep, no more; and by a sleep to say we end the heartache and the thousand natural shocks that flesh is heir to: 'tis a consummation devoutly to be wish'd. To die, to sleep; to sleep, perchance to dream.* But then again arises the philosophical dilemma, because if we die and go to sleep, then what dreams will come in that sleep of death? We stay alive because we don't know for sure what death will bring. We choose to suffer because we fear the unknown alternative. But really – on an everyday level of life – we suffer because we don't dare ask the uncomfortable questions; because we don't dare the conversation. We suffer because we don't communicate.

Where is this world heading? Where are we heading as humans? Western civilisation stands on a knife edge, with everything to lose. We are standing at the edge, staring into the abyss of chaos being the annihilation of the very bedrock of democracy. It will be the end of democracy if freedom of speech is forever inhibited by the fear of offense, and if we allow our own technological advancements to control how we identify with each other.

30

THE I, WE, AND THEY

Do you feel all motivated now? Do you feel inspired now? Do you feel ready to take to the stage, rise and let your voice be heard? Good. Then where do we start? Do you feel like you know exactly how to put these 50.000 words you have just read into use? No? Really? I'm so disappointed. No, I'm kidding. I get it. It's a lot to take in. I have not forgotten my promise to you from the beginning. *By the end of this book, you will not only feel inspired to find a voice of your own but know how to create a message that people will not ignore.* Did you do what I suggested and turn every chapter in ideas for your own speech? Let's turn your ideas into a speech.

It's summary time!

1. If you actually want to make an impact, first know that you have to be comfortable with what you see in the mirror. The good, the bad and the ugly.
2. What is your strategic purpose; what is your

personal reason for getting up there do that speech/presentation/Ted talk?

3. Decide on one topic. Not five. And know why this will be your speech.

4. Craft your speech according to the trinity: Ethos, Pathos, and Logos. The first five minutes of a 30-minute speech is ethos. Why You? What is your credibility for talking about this subject? Next 20 minutes is pathos. Make them emotionally connect with you about the topic. Make them care. Make them interested. Last five minutes are logos. What is your core message? Conclusion. What do they take away?

5. Draw the treasure map of your speech and memorise the image of the map. If you tell a personal story, trust that you know your own story. If you're asked by your boss to do a presentation, you're not asked to talk about something you know nothing about. You know what you're talking about. Just decide what it is and put it on the map, so you know where it is. Write nothing down. Draw it!

6. While preparing your delivery, you could consider voice, anchoring and all the fancy tricks, but before you get experienced enough to pull that off with competence, it's much more efficient to focus on what those three parts should achieve. How do you make them trust you? How do you make them care, and finally, how do you make them understand your message? In the beginning you get a lot further with a general focus on whether you have their attention than you do with the tricks.

7. The one tip for delivery: Vary your pace! Don't

plan the pauses. Don't talk slowly on purpose. Vary your pace and speed up when you can. Otherwise, just stay in it. Feel it.

8. Prepare your mental story of how your speech will unfold and be received to create the potential for success. Make sure fear of the stage does not catch you off guard.

9. Get up there and do exactly what you had envisioned in your mental preparation. Witness your best-case scenario unfold and enjoy the nerves, the jitters, and the random shakes.

For now, that's it. What?... I know, I know, I know, relax. Breathe. You say: *I get the trinity. I get the ethos, pathos, logos part. I mean, I understand it. I want to be like Jesus, the best speaker of all time* (kidding), *and I think I know how to put the speech together. How to structure the speech. But I still feel like I don't know what to do about me. If I don't prepare anything in terms of pauses or vocal variety or anchoring, then what am I supposed to do up there. I can't go up there not knowing what to do, because I am not good at it. What about ME?* I know, my friend. You want the *10 Easy Steps: How To Become a World-Class Speaker*. I'm sorry, my friend. I won't do that to you. I will not leave you to mediocrity and a fake sense of safety. It's one of the most daunting things in the world to speak in front of a crowd of people. I won't lie to you. It is. We are frail, insecure, doubtful beings. But your best chance of fucking yourself up completely is getting distracted by having prepared too much of a show. You don't need 10 different things to do to pull off a competent speech. It's a subtle art. An art of words, presence, flirting, eye contact, connection and interest. You can master the tricks like anchoring and VAK range over time, but first, just get them to bloody pay attention. Be personal. Stay in the present of your speech and think about what you're saying and to who. That's why I'm going to give you my secret sauce. This is my secret recipe. It sounds a little Narnia-esque and is called:

The *I*, the *We*, and the *They*

It's a bit like the law of attraction; what you think about will happen. It's not rocket-science really, but it's effective, and you have no idea how many times I've used it to walk on stage having made no decisions whatsoever about what I would do with myself, while up there. It's like Aristotle's trinity of rhetoric, but where ethos, pathos and logos are focused on your speech and what you say, the *I*, *We* and *They* focus on you and what you're doing. *Ethos, pathos, logos* is about what you are saying, and with which words you choose to do so. The *I*, *We* and *They* is the energy with which you approach them. It's your own state of mind.

Let's take a 30-minute speech again as an example. While we focus the first 5 minutes of your material on your ethos, simultaneously, you focus on *I*. Where am I in this topic? Where am I in this situation that is unfolding between me and the listeners? Your next 20 minutes is your pathos being communicated. At the same time, you focus on *we*. Where are *we* in this speech? You and them. Where is the common ground? How can you and they connect as a *we* about your story and about this topic? Finally, for the last 5 minutes, while you communicate your logos, your full focus is on them. Where are *they* in your message? How are *they* affected by your message? How much do you want for them? Be there, with the message, for them.

I know it is difficult to believe that you should do so seemingly little, but that is what all the best speakers in the world and all the best actors in the world do. They focus on something much more general, much more ethereal, much more universal. They focus on being present and for whom. They don't speak or perform. They serve! They have practiced and practiced, done all the mocking about with the tricks and rehearsals, but when it's showtime, all of that preparation must disappear, so you can shine through. Just get up there and know perfection does not exist. You are not supposed to be a superstar. You are supposed to start, and one day it will be second nature to you.

Five minutes of *I*. 20 minutes of *We*, and five minutes of *They*. What you will find is that a lot of the tricks you could have decided to use consciously will happen anyway, because your body is pulled to act in a certain way as a result of your mind's focus. Your body is aligned with a focused mind. This is what you do, when you don't know what to do about yourself. You, figuratively, post-it these three words in the back of your mind like mental cue cards to the orchestra for the music to change. Whatever comes out of your mouth, you have this tiny word inside your head. It calms and centres yourself on stage, because your body is not tempted to opt for one of the thousands of insane ideas your brain can up with, within 30 minutes, about what you could do. *Maybe I should sit. Maybe I should stand. Maybe I should shout suddenly. Maybe I should laugh more. Maybe I should run across the stage. Maybe I should close my eyes and then open them in a slow and dramatic way. Maybe I should do the imaginary brick... or the horizontal pyramid. Maybe...* All of that internal chaos is silenced by one simple but constant focus. *I... We... They...*

31

A NEW TRINITY

I'VE ALWAYS BEEN UTTERLY FASCINATED by the Holy Trinity of Christianity. Not for the sake of its religious content, but because of the legacy it has left us. We have a vast treasure trove of art and literature that we owe to the dubious promotion of the Holy Trinity. And by dubious, I mean the motivation for the promotion and means by which it was promoted having been questionable – to say the least. None-theless, the structure of the Father, the Son and the Holy Spirit is incredible as it relates to communication. I hope you feel that way too by now. But the trinity is just the tip of the iceberg. For all its short-comings Christianity has also inspired more than a thousand years of search for love, morals, a better life and the good in man. Nowhere is this more generously delivered than through art and literature. We now have thousands upon thousands of ancient writings to document the history of human communication that we can attribute to the search for a higher meaning in life. Also, we would not have Rembrandt's beautiful painting The Storm, teaching about the courage to venture into the unknown, were it not for the Trinity. We would not have

Michelangelo's splendour of the Sistine chapel, or Da Vinci's Madonna of the Rocks or Marco D'agrate's haunting statue of the flayed St. Bartholomew were it not for the Greek philosopher's quest for truth and meaning, Jesus' message of love or the astounding communicative powers of the Holy Trinity.

But times have moved on. It's time for a new trinity, when it comes to communication. We have moved on. It's time for an update. So, why don't we take all the good that has been passed on to us; the incredibly effective structure of Aristotle's trinity, the moral and ethical depths of love from the Holy Trinity, the emotional swoop of the dramatic trinity, with its three acts; beginning, middle and end, and forge it all into a 21st century trinity. I gave it to you in the beginning in its simplest form:

1. Get skilled as a public speaker (*I*)
2. Dare to be honest and assume you will offend some, in the name of curiosity and understanding (*We*)
3. Get your purpose straight. (*They*)

If you build this simple trinity into every statement you make, being a five sentence SoMe post, a 20-minute TEDx Talk, a wedding speech or a 60-minute presentation at work, you are bound to connect with your audience. Whoever they might be. Let us unite under this new trinity. A modern trinity with a new father, a new son, and the eternally present spirit. And why we're at it, why not a new creed?

A CREED OF COMMUNICATION

The New Father:
I believe in getting skilled as a communicator, and I believe in credibility and taking responsibility for the ethos of my communication.
(The ethos. The *I*)

The New Son:
I believe in the courage and the commitment to be honest and personal with my message and assume I will offend some, for do I not offend anyone, then my message is not important enough. I shall not offend purposefully, but communicate with kindness, respect and curiosity. I wow to be personal in life and business and shall not take it personally if criticised.
(The pathos. The *We*)

The New Spirit:
I believe in the purpose of my message to be truly for the benefit of others and not because I am addicted to the likes or the attention. I wow to always hold the light of true purpose; to seek connection; to let my voice be heard so others my find theirs.
(The logos. The *They*)

Indeed!

WHEN ALL ELSE FAILS

FINALLY, I guess you could ask, what is the one thing that a speaker must possess above all? That one thing, if all else fails, that will still make you stand out and make you memorable to the listeners. Let me give you one final brief story about an American modern-dance choreographer called Paul Taylor. A documentary film was made about his life years ago. *The Dance Maker.* He had his dance company, based in the heart of New York City for years, and in the film, there's a scene where they cut to a few ensemble dancers suddenly discussing their shock to realise that one of their friends and colleagues, a fellow dancer in the company has been fired. They don't understand the decision. They found the friend to be both talented and pleasant. Cut to the principal dancers, who were more distanced acknowledging that that is simply part of the game. Cut to the choreographer and now former employer of the dancer who says something like this:

"I took her into the B-company under the assumption that she would develop into the A-company. Somehow, she never really developed. I don't know. She just wasn't interesting."

And just like that, with a ruthless bombshell of honesty, the dancer was out. At the end of the day, when all else fails, be interesting. At the end of the day, it's not about talent or skill or personal drive. No one will ever hire you, if they don't find you interesting. No one will listen to you if they don't find you interesting.

I know there are some out there who will honestly say: *But I'm not interesting.* To them I say, *really? Are you serious? After everything we have been through, you're going to pull that one me NOW. I am so disappointed. And I will slap you the next time I see you. Lovingly.* When it comes to being interesting, you have one incredible advantage going for you. One that very few people actually use as an advantage, because they may not even be aware of it. It requires great skill, experience, and cunning use of drama to be interesting, without also being personal. Being personal means being You, and you were born the World Champion at being You – many people just lose sight of that in their daily quest to compare themselves with everyone else. I will bet you everything I own, that dancer in the Paul Taylor Company was found uninteresting, because she stopped being herself, caught up in a daily competition with the other dancers, and ended up a poor, bland, mediocre version of someone else. There is no one in the world better at being You than you. No one can be that unique individual that you are like you can. If you start to use this fact with awareness, being interesting suddenly becomes quite easy, because you can set yourself apart from the crowd, simply being something that no one else on the planet can be. You. You are the f... World Champion. USE IT!

You are nothing as a speaker, if you are not interesting, and you can't be interesting if you are not personal. When you communicate, whether it being on social media, from a podium or a stage, no one can ignore you; no one will stop paying attention to you, if you show them something no one else on the planet can. Be yourself. Be personal. There is your value.

EPILOGUE

Here's the rub

OUR BIGGEST ASSET collectively as a human race is **diversity**, and I will put forth to you that understanding diversity is our greatest tool in not only leadership and marketing, but our ability to communicate as humans. We all have distinct personalities and if we learn to both accept and understand the diversity of human personality, then we have an incredible potential to get the right messages out into the world. The messages that can and should change the world because they will touch everybody. Getting your video seen on social media is not just about a clever marketing strategy. It's about understanding diversity; understanding that we all have different personalities, different upbringings, different cultural backgrounds and different gender identities. We may not all look the same, but we all feel the same and we all hurt the same.

I went on stage for the wrong reasons. Because I was

addicted to attention, and putting an attention addicted young man directly in a leading role is like going from smoking Marlboro lights straight to shooting heroin every night, with a thousand people giving you a standing ovation, while doing it. I went on stage, having misunderstood completely what communication is all about. It did not spell the end of me. Fortunately, I learned that communication is neither speaking nor getting attention, but having people around you honest enough to tell your truth back to you. This is where I return to my opening quote, and my favourite quote of all time:

"The single biggest problem in communication is the illusion that it has taken place." – George Bernard Shaw

We're stuck behind screens writing volumes of utterances that we would never say to each other if we were face-to-face, under the illusion that we communicate. But it is face-to-face that life begins. It's in the interaction that we become human. That we feel truly alive. We can't avoid social media. That would be foolish and naïve to expect. But we can learn to use social media effectively and consciously.

Did I manage to offend you along the way? Oh, I certainly hope so. First, because I didn't mean to hurt you with malevolent will. Second, if I offended you at any point, it means some of this is as important to you as it is to me. If so, I do hope you try to explain your point of view to me with as much care as I have put into writing this book.

This is what it all comes down to for me. This is my definition of communication, and the one quote that I hope you will make a meme out of with a picture of my looking very insightful. Here it is:

"The core of communication is a response. A response of understanding an intent. You have not communicated until you have heard the retelling of your own words ring true to your ears." - *Martin Svaneborg*

This is it, my dear friends. It's the end of line. What's there left to say? Some of us are meant to be speakers. Some are meant to be in the audience, but all of us have a story of value to someone else, and all of us can raise our game a little. We do not reserve the world of public speaking for a handful of superstar speakers. The important messages will not out unless we all become better; unless we all pick up the torch, carry forth the mantle of ambition for communicating a little more competently, respectfully and with a little more integrity in our everyday lives. Imagine what the world would look like if everybody became just 10% better speakers. We actually could change the world, but will we? Do we actually need the obstacles and the problems to have a good enough reason to get up in the morning?

One thing is for sure. You will never be happy, if you're not something to someone, and even if you don't feel like you have anyone in your life, you can always reach out and be something for someone. You can always ask someone a question that will make them feel seen; that will make their day. The same goes for speakers. If you're up there for selfish reasons, you're basically just a crazy person talking to yourself. You're not a public speaker unless you are up there for them. The ones out there in the dark.

Some of us are extroverts. Some of us are introverts. Many are on the ever-sliding grey-scale in between. Whether you take to the stage or listen from the darkness, you are important to someone, and you deserve recognition for that;

for the fact that you get up in the morning and try to make sense of it all; for the fact that you had enough ambition about yourself to pick up this book, let alone finish it; for the fact that you're still here. Well done. Now, go forth and communicate with curiosity, and the world will only get better. Chose to understand a perspective other than your own. We need that. Because… none of us are anything, if we are nothing to no one.

The end.

BONUS MATERIAL

Appendix A

Conversation exercises

Here is **how to have a better conversation of opinion:** The acclaimed psychologist, Carl Rogers came up with a great exercise on how to enhance your conversational skills. It goes like this:

Make an exercise by constituting this rule: Before stating an opinion or statement of your own, you have to repeat the statement of the other speaker before you, to the satisfaction of the other speaker.

It will prevent the conversation from being a competition for dominance and being right, and develop the conversation to one of listening, learning and understanding. You will learn how to listen on a whole new level, because you have to not only pay attention, but listen so carefully to another person's viewpoint that you can retell it as your own. It is much more difficult than you might imagine, and so incredibly rewarding.

Amazing party game for conversation: One person has to tell a personal story in 2-3 minutes. Something like your first kiss, or your most embarrassing moment, always gets the fun going in an interesting way. Then the person next to you has to retell your story accurately. After the retelling, that person then shares a story of their own, which, in turn, is retold by the next person, and so on and so forth. You have no idea how a group can bond in a matter of twenty minutes, and how much everyone will have raised their capacity for listening.

––––––

Appendix B

Questions & Answers

Before I bid thee a fond farewell, until the next time, I have collected a few questions received, after trusted readers have read the first draft of this book.

Question about criterion #1. Distractions:

"I totally see how I can fall into these traps of distracting, but I am not sure how I would notice, whether I fail to meet this criterion. How do I make sure I noticed my own distraction mistakes?"

Answer:

"It is a somewhat vague area to check up on, as it relies on your capacity for self-awareness. The best way to check yourself to see if you are making distraction mistakes, is actually to check your audience. Look at them. Are they paying attention? Are they with you? If you feel you have their attention, then you are not distracting them. It is difficult to check your own mistakes, but it is quite easy to check the result of them.

Question about authenticity:

"What if you have no problem turning the dark corners of your past inside out? How can you then challenge yourself to further develop your authenticity?

Answer:

"That could easily turn into a quite deep and spiritual conversation, which I will not go into here. I will say though, if you are fine with talking about the darkness of your past, then trust that you are also able to be authentic when needed. However, the example I mentioned about the girl telling the personal story about her controlling sister, the point was that when she had to step back into that memory and re-live the emotions of that memory, she was not as fine with the darkness as she thought. So, I would say, if you get a chance to practise your personal stories in front of others, then challenge yourself to stop, when you are in the middle of that story. Take time to think about it; remember; re-live it. See the memories before you and feel if you are really at ease with the painful emotion of the dark memory. If you are, great, but more often we are not. In that case, we have to spend time with our dark memories. If you have personal stories that you know you want to use in you speaking, then find time to practise telling those stories out loud to yourself, and in the comfort of your solitude, take time to really re-live the moments and the emotions connected to them.

The test of your knowledge about the country of Denmark. Did you pass?

"Ugly ducklings turned into beautiful swans..."

Reference to the fairytale The Ugly Duckling, written by Hans Christian Andersen in the nineteenth century. Congratulations. You are on par with a fourth grader.

"Life is understood backwards but must be lived forwards."

A famous statement by the eccentric, existentialist philosopher, Søren Kierkegaard, who lived at the same time and only a stone's throw from H.C. Andersen, and coincidentally reviewed one of Andersen's very first publications. I am genuinely impressed and thrilled if you knew that one. We could hang out.

"princes in ancient castles lamented over life and death; being or not being, while holding up skulls in wonder..."

Yes, Sherlock, this is of course a reference to the opening line of the famous soliloquy *To be or not to be*, written by William Shakespeare about the troubled Prince Hamlet living in the historic Kronborg Castle, which is in the lovely town of Elsinore about an hour north of the capitol of Denmark, Copenhagen. Every year they perform a production of Hamlet in this very castle, where the story takes place. Productions which have featured all-star hamlets like the iconic Lawrence Oliver/Vivian Leigh 1937 production in the courtyard of Kronborg Castle to subsequent Hamlets like John Gielgud, Richard Burton, Christopher Plummer, Michael Caine and Jude Law.

ABOUT THE AUTHOR

With a background in musical theatre as both an actor, singer, and dancer, Martin Svaneborg has spent his teenage and adult life as a storyteller. In 2018, driven mainly by his interest in the history of religion, Martin started studying theology at the University of Copenhagen while exploring other ways of telling stories as a theatre director, speech coach, and speaker, hence the transition to novel writing felt natural, and his debut novel, A Moment Of Faith will be published in 2021. It is a fusion of his growing interest for the personal life of the philosophers he encountered during his studies and the desire to tell an adventurous love story.

You can always find Martin at his website:

www.martinsvaneborgtalks.com

 facebook.com/MartinSvaneborgAuthor
instagram.com/martinsvaneborg

A famous philosopher. A forgotten church, and a theology
student scared of conflict.

coming in the summer of 2021

A MOMENT OF FAITH

"Cast off the deed of darkness and put on the armour of light."

Copenhagen, 1840 – Consumed by a suppressed animosity towards the Church, nonconformist philosopher, Søren Kierkegaard, rushes rashly through the cobbled streets , thrusting himself into a love story with disastrous repercussions.

Copenhagen, 1855 – Withering away in a lone hospital bed, in an attempt to achieve immortality, Kierkegaard conjures a preposterous plan to take down not only the established Church of Denmark but Christianity itself.

Copenhagen, Now – Wandering into a church belonging to a vanishing branch of Christianity, theology student and introvert Christian Kardahl meets devout and mysterious Emma for the first time. Two days later, and by sheer coincidence, Christian comes across a letter by Søren Kierkegaard, delivering a message that could either heal or destroy the Christian Faith. He and Emma are consequently drawn into an involuntary quest that takes them all the way to the very birthplace of the apostles.

———————

Join Martin's READER CLUB by following the link below, and get notified of future book releases.

https://author.martinsvaneborgtalks.com/martin-svaneborg-author